A SIMPLE and EFFECTIVE CURE for CRIMINALITY

A SIMPLE and EFFECTIVE CURE for CRIMINALITY

A *PSYCHOLOGICAL* DETECTIVE STORY

REG REYNOLDS AND
DOUGLAS QUIRK

To order additional copies of this book, contact:
Xlibris
1-888-795-4274
www.Xlibris.com
Orders@Xlibris.com
788817

A SIMPLE AND EFFECTIVE CURE FOR CRIMINALITY[1]

A Psychological Detective Story

Reg Reynolds and Douglas Quirk
with Verna Nutbrown

Executive Summary

---

[1] An abbreviated version of this paper, Assessment And Large-Group Treatment Of Criminality, was presented at the annual meeting of the Mental Health in Corrections Consortium, Kansas City, MO., 1996. Here, we need to distinguish between criminality, the psychological state that predisposed one to commit crimes (and which can be treated psychologically), and crime itself, the end result of that disposition.

We would like to thank the Ontario Ministry of Correctional Services and our various Superintendents and Regional Directors, without whose support none of this work could have been done. Their interest in the correctional process has been an inspiration and is largely responsible for the decision to pursue the study of criminality described below. Acknowledgement is also due to two individual volunteers who selflessly gave of their time and effort to perform many of the tasks involved in this work, Linda Delmedico and Nicole Pekmezaris. Many thanks to all.

The opinions and positions expressed in this paper are those of the authors, and don't necessarily represent the opinions of any other organizations or individuals.

A ten-year research project to understand and treat criminality has led to the development of a new test of criminal thinking, Survey of Thoughts, Feelings and Behaviours (STFB), [2] [3] and a new understanding of criminality as six sets of angry distress-rejecting attitudes and behaviours on the part of offenders − behaviours which put them into conflict with society and get them in trouble with the law. This new understanding of criminality suggested the development of six different treatment programs, one for each of these six separate components of criminality; and these treatment programs were delivered in six day-long (i.e., 4½ hour) large-group treatment workshops. None of those inmates who were assigned to and received three or more of these treatment workshops recidivated (i.e., relapsed into crime) within the two years following release from prison − in contrast to a control group of inmates who received none of these criminality workshops, half of whom were back in prison within two years of being released. It was concluded that this particular approach to understanding and treating criminality would seem to warrant further investigation and application.

---

[2]   See Appendix A for the STFB questionnaire and scoring procedure.
[3]   Copyright R.M. Reynolds 1996.

CONTENTS

A SIMPLE AND EFFECTIVE CURE FOR CRIMINALITY[4]

"Research is not done the way people who write books about research say that it is done."

— Bachrach's First Law of Research

In a way, this is a detective story. Oh, it doesn't have the excitement of explosions, gun fire and demolition-derby police chases, nor does it have the benefit of fear of imminent danger with stalking

[4] An abbreviated version of this paper, Assessment And Large-Group Treatment Of Criminality, was presented at the annual meeting of the Mental Health in Corrections Consortium, Kansas City, MO., 1996. Here, we need to distinguish between criminality, the psychological state that predisposed one to commit crimes (and which can be treated psychologically), and crime itself, the end result of that disposition.

We would like to thank the Ontario Ministry of Correctional Services and our various Superintendents and Regional Directors, without whose support none of this work could have been done. Their interest in the correctional process has been an inspiration and is largely responsible for the decision to pursue the study of criminality described below. Acknowledgement is also due to two individual volunteers who selflessly gave of their time and effort to perform many of the tasks involved in this work, Linda Delmedico and Nicole Pekmezaris. Many thanks to all.

The opinions and positions expressed in this paper are those of the authors, and don't necessarily represent the opinions of any other organizations or individuals.

killers and maniacal sex fiends with which to spice up the tale, as in media melodramas. Nor do we have the charisma of handsome and dashing young detectives rushing in to save endangered victims at the last moment. No, this story is one of a pair of old stick-in-the-muds, without even uniforms to enhance our images or the public street as a setting in which real people live, plodding rather too meticulously through mounds of information, trying to find solutions to a crime which has puzzled humankind for centuries.

But what is the crime this farce of bumbling defectives is setting out to solve? The answer to this question depends to some extent on who you are. How we perceive anything depends heavily on our point of view. For example, if you are one who is puzzled by the problem, "Why do people perform crimes? – then the "crime" we are trying to solve is that of crime itself. If you are one who is puzzled about what to do about crime and criminals – then the "crime" we are trying to solve is how to understand and correct criminals, and even how to prevent crime. If you are one who wishes to prevent yourself or a loved one from performing crimes in the future – then the "crime" we are trying to solve is a crime that has not yet happened, and our goal would be to offer a solid basis for hope that it will not happen. If you are one who believes the government or the justice system is not doing enough of the right things to protect the citizenry from the growing wave of violence and eradicate the dangers we all face each day – then the "crime" we are addressing is concerned with the errors that the justice system has been making and how those errors might be corrected. The list of points of view is almost endless. So, you see, the nature of the crime at issue depends to some extent on your point of view. But, since we cannot guess what your point of view may be, obviously we have to adopt as general a point of view as possible, so that some basis is provided for each reader to feel that his or her point of view gets fair attention.

If we aren't going to tell you exactly what the crime is, how are we going to tell the story about its solution? Well, as we have already hinted, the story will sound quite a lot like what really happens in real-life detective work. In real-life detective work, the task involves long hours, days, weeks and months of plodding relentlessly through piles of information on a wide range of cases, all of which have to be investigated, to sort out real leads from false ones, to cross-check people's statements, to make guesses and interpretations about what happened and then to tear them down, to try out various methods of reconstructing and examining scraps of evidence, to search, and to search again for new facts, and so on. The story about any such real-life enterprise is not likely to carry the reader lightly through a few entertaining hours. But it can be deeply engrossing, and it can offer the reader a chance to participate actively in examining the evidence and in reaching a real understanding of the problem and his or her own conclusions about the nature and prevention of the crime in question.

Still, before we start to tell this detective story, we must try to be clear about the "section of the department" (in a real police force this would refer to sections such as homicide or vice) in which we work – that is, the kinds of issues we will and will not be addressing.

If you ask almost anybody to tell you about criminality, you are likely to awaken images of tough and macho, or sneaky and sleazy, men whose lives are selfishly committed to taking advantage of others, acts of violence, images of murder and terrorism, images of silent conspiracies and stashes of weapons and drugs, images of police chases and shoot-outs, and perhaps images of helpless women unable to escape from sexual slavery and enforced prostitution, or even of courtroom dramas and the bars of prison cells. Surely, these are what crime is about. Actually, of course, these are merely images from the imaginations of the media people to which we have been exposed repeatedly. These images have very little in common with real crime, criminals or criminality, and we will not be addressing them, at least directly. What we will be doing is assessing and treating the cognitive and affective motivations that "drive" criminal behaviour, in an attempt to cure and prevent criminality.

The Context of This Research

This assessment and treatment program was carried out within the Ontario Correctional Institute (OCI), a modern 220-bed medium security prison opened in late 1973. The OCI's inmate population was composed primarily of alcoholics, drug addicts and sex offenders, all of whom were serving "provincial" sentences. In Ontario, this means that their maximum imposed sentence was two years less a day, plus any additional probation time which may have been imposed at the time of sentencing. Few of these inmates were considered to be "career criminals," although a majority of them were recidivists at the time of their admission to the OCI, with significant numbers exhibiting long histories of criminal involvements of many types.

The OCI's mission statement commits it and all of its staff to assessment, treatment, training, safe confinement of adult male incarcerated offenders, and research. As the premier correctional treatment setting in Ontario, it had been charged specifically with the task of exploring criminality as it is related to its inmate population. And what an interesting task that has turned out to be!

Historical Background

In 1976, shortly after the OCI opened, Samuel Yochelson, Director of the Program for the Investigation of Criminal Behaviour at St. Elizabeth's Hospital in Washington, D.C., and Stanton Samenow, a clinical research psychologist, published the results of a study of criminal thinking in which they claimed to have identified the errors of thinking that characterize the criminal mind. In this publication, they divided the thinking errors that they had observed into three broad clusters. The first cluster, composed of 16 thinking errors, they called "Criminal Thinking Patterns." A second cluster of thinking errors was labelled "Automatic Errors of Thinking," while a third cluster of thinking errors, "From Idea Through Execution," was concerned with the actual execution of criminal activity. These three clusters and the behaviours they subsume seemed to have a certain face validity and, regardless of whether or not these characteristics really portrayed criminal thinking or whether they were merely general attributions that could be acknowledged by many other people as well, workers in the criminal justice system were quick to recognize in these descriptions the offenders with whom they were familiar.

A year after their treatise on the criminal mind, Yochelson and Samenow (1977) published a description of a treatment program they designed to modify these supposedly criminalistic patterns of thought and behaviour. In so doing, they were following the cognitive tradition which has become identified with Ellis (1962), Meichenbaum (1977) and Beck (Beck, Rushton, Shaw and Emory, 1979), and which was destined to become the bandwagon of the 1980's and beyond.

Their treatment program placed the criminal in "a group with three to five participants. Attendance in this group every weekday is part of a disciplined life in which time is programmed. ... *The group meets for three hours a day, five days a week, for at least a year.*" [italics added] (Yochelson and Samenow, Vol II, pp. 179, 180). Their work was primarily cognitive: "In summary, we work with the raw data of thinking. We extract thinking errors, establishing the fact that each error is part of a broader criminal pattern. We teach the criminal new corrective, responsible thinking patterns here and now, and prepare him for future situations." (op. cit., p. 176). Success was reported in terms such as the following: "As of May 1976, thirteen men who were hard-core criminals are now living in the community and fulfil our strict criteria of responsible functioning." (op. cit., p. 436).

In 1986, Anupama Bhardwaj (later Bhardwaj-Keats), a student intern at the OCI, decided to test the validity of Yochelson and Samenow's observations by attempting to construct a paper-and-pencil psychological test to measure forty-six of the criminal thinking errors that they had "identified." This research, which subsequently became her doctoral dissertation, demonstrated a robust difference in the scores obtained on her test by normal community college students and by men incarcerated in provincial correctional facilities. That is, *she demonstrated that*, in Yochelson and Samenow's terms, *not only the criminally insane, but "garden variety" incarcerates as well, could be said to possess "the criminal mind."*

Development of the Survey of Thoughts, Feelings and Behaviours (STFB)

Nevertheless, there were a few problems with the test that Bhardwaj had developed. Some of the items were sexist. For example, one of the items read, "My idea of good sex is to conquer a woman's body," which would seem to make it less than ideal for use with females. Another item was, "When I'm doing crime, I've more energy than most people," which would seem to presuppose what the test might be attempting to discover. In an attempt to produce a measure of criminal thinking that might be used for clinical purposes, therefore, the present authors repeated and extended the test development process which had been followed by Bhardwaj-Keats; and *over the next five years*, items were written and either retained or discarded depending upon their ability to differentiate between successive samples of Normals and Criminals. The eighth and final version of this new test, designated a "Survey of Thoughts, Feelings and Behaviours" (STFB), contains only two of Bhardwaj-Keats' original 181 items in their original form, and another dozen or so in altered form. It consists of one hundred items – two items for each of fifty different kinds of "thinking errors," one of which is scored if answered in the True direction while the other is scored if answered in the False direction.

Next, fifty students from a university psychology class were asked to rate the STFB items for their social desirability, using a seven-point scale ranging from Very Socially Desirable to Very Socially Undesirable. From among those items judged to be relatively neutral with respect to Social Desirability (mean ratings between 3.5 and 4.5), sixteen items were selected such that eight of the items were scored if answered in the True direction and eight were scored if answered in the False direction. The mean Social Desirability rating for these 16 items was 4.00. In a similar way, from among those items rated by the university students as "very socially undesirable," another sixteen items were selected. Again, half of these items were scored if answered in the True direction, and half were scored if answered False. The mean rating for these items on the seven-point scale of social desirability was 5.8

Factor Structure and Meaning in the STFB

Factor analysis of the fifty 2-item sets of "thinking errors" comprising the STFB produced an acceptable six factor solution that accounted for 67 percent of the variance in a sample of 355 inmate subjects and which, with a slight adjustment for content, resulted in six interpretable "factor scales" having satisfactory internal consistencies (alpha's ranging from 0.75 to 0.85).

STFB factor scale scores and MMPI[5] data were then obtained for a separate sample of 340 inmate subjects, and MMPI item endorsements were determined for subjects who scored high – at or above a T-score of 65 – on each of the STFB factor scales. Then, assembling together the items from each of the six STFB factors along with the MMPI items associated with high scores on each, the six sets of STFB and MMPI items were characterized in terms of the possible developmental sequence of both the cognitive and reactive mechanisms (the STFB items) and the motivational and psychopathological features (the MMPI items) common to each array, which provided a more refined understanding of the psychodynamics underlying each of the criminality factors than could have been obtained from examination of the items in each of the STFB factors alone.

---

[5]   The Minnesota Multifactor Personality Inventory (MMPI) is a well-known personality test.

Postulated Psychodynamics of the STFB

The postulated psychodynamics portrayed the six factors as representing a series of reactions to perceived life experiences, the internal processing of which eventuates in various forms of *angry distress-rejecting reactions* on the part of offenders, as follows:

Factor 1: Hypersensitivity to and rejection of feelings of Guilt

Factor 2: Hypersensitivity to and rejection of feelings of Failure

Factor 3: Hypersensitivity to and rejection of Emotional Distress

Factor 4: Hypersensitivity to and rejection of Sensitivity to Others

Factor 5: Hypersensitivity to and rejection of Closeness

Factor 6: Hypersensitivity to and rejection of Discipline

For purpose of illustration, the postulated psychodynamics for the first STFB factor (hypersensitivity to and rejection of feelings of guilt) are

a) One or more significant others was perceived by the child as overemphasizing the child's mistakes and wrongdoing.
b) The child reacted with a sense of rejection, sensitivity to guilt, and a readiness to feel guilty.
c) The child accepted the felt guilt and felt rejection, and reacted with a kind of compulsive cautiousness, with depressive overtones, which led to some inhibition of activity.
d) The felt rejection, combined with the inhibition of activity and energy use, fostered in the child a build-up of resentment and anger at the perceived injustice of his situation, feelings which also could not be expressed too directly.
e) The combination of guilt and anger feelings created strong negative feelings about emotions, with a suppression of

emotions – which suppression, in turn, may have led to boredom. Nevertheless, the anger could not be suppressed fully, and it was evoked particularly by the elicitation of guilt feelings which were immediately rejected.

f) The elicitation of guilt and anger feelings created increased Autonomic Nervous System (ANS) arousal that, with the rejection of guilt, seemed to override the previous inhibition of action. The result involved a heightened excitability of the person, an increased intensity of anger, and a search for relief in excitement-seeking activities, some of which others might consider would lead naturally to feelings of guilt.

g) The excitement seeking and/or the angry pursuit of action that normally might be considered guilt-evoking enhanced the risk of involvement in criminal behaviour.

h) In effect, the individual seems to be saying, "I refuse to feel guilty about what I do! In fact, I am going to do whatever the hell I please, and I'll show you that I don't feel guilty about it."

Designing the Treatment Programs

Based on the understanding of criminal thinking outlined above, day-long programs were designed to address the motivations presumed to be underlying each of the six criminal thinking factors; these day-long programs were presented in large-group treatment workshop format; and changes in factor scale scores from before to after treatment were examined to determine our success in modifying criminal thinking.

The six separate treatment-of-criminal-thinking workshop programs (each one addressing a different criminal thinking factor)[6] were developed, as follows:

1. Guilt was the target of the first workshop (Enjoying Criticism), and the attempt was to be made to reduce the amount of guilt feeling and guilt proneness, on the assumption that this would

---

[6] For reasons peripheral to the treatment of these specific criminal thinking factors, but as part of a larger treatment research project, these six criminal thinking workshops were supplemented by two "Values" workshops, as follows:

Values Re-ordering is the topic of this workshop, and the attempt is made to re-order values – assuming this will reduce rebellion against "external" controls. Section methods are

   a) **Orientation to Values' Structure**: Orientation to the structure of values. Listing personal values.
   b) **Imagery characteristics**: The nature of reality and its images. Changing image sub-modalities.
   c) **Altering Position of Values**: Sub-modalities shifting and restructuring values. Re-evaluation of values.
   d) **Relaxation & Imagery**: Relaxation training. Relaxed consideration of constructed images (life style, relaxed personality, social competence, etc.)

Values Healing is the topic of this workshop, and the attempt is made to correct conflicted values images – assuming that this will reduce rebellion against "internal" controls. Section methods are

   a. **Orientation to Values**: Values orientation. Listing of personal values. Values images.
   b. **Squash**: Healing conflicted values.
   c. **Time Line & Relisting Values**: Time-Line trips to find source beliefs and review them. Relist values.
   d. **Squash**: More healing of conflicted values, with Programming-Relaxation.

have the effect of reducing guilt intolerance. Methods to be used[7] in each section of the day were

a) **Orientation to Guilt Feelings**: Guilt as an after-the-fact self-judgement when things could not have been different. All are perfect. Guilt unnecessary. Time in good vs. bad.

b) **Reframing**: Negative format and guilt tripping. How do you make yourself feel guilty? Semantics of guilt talk. Time-Line[8] to a guilt-evoking event – walk through it. Swish for a guilt-evoking image.

c) **Squash & Relaxation**: Squash for Guilt/Innocence, Bad/Good, Crime/Being Straight. Relaxation training.

d) **Desensitization**: Phobia Cure & more Time-Line for guilt-tripping, criticism, feeling guilty.

2. Failure was the target of the second workshop, and the attempt was made to reduce the amount of failure feeling and failure proneness, on the assumption that this will have the effect of reducing failure intolerance. Methods for each section of the day were

a) **Orientation to Failure Feelings:** Failure as a result of incorporation of others' judgements. You never failed except to meet others' inappropriate standards for you. Effort here is

---

[7]   It became necessary to change the content of the first workshop slightly during the workshop itself. In principle that is not good. However, it is sometimes necessary to respond to the needs of the group (in this case, many questions), to the actual flow of how we are doing, and to the sense we have of the therapeutics involved. So, since many "didn't get it" during the first Time-Line operation, we did a second Time-Line operation later in place of the planned Rational Emotive Therapy (RET).

[8]   Time-Line, Squash, Swish, and Phobia Cure are all Neuro-Linguistic Programming procedures and may be found in James and Woodsmall (1987) and Andreas & Andreas (1989). Reframing, while not unique to NLP, may be found in Bandler & Grinder (1982).

     to reduce failure feelings/proneness. Reframing: Assumption of need to compete.

b) **How do you** make yourself feel like a failure? Semantics of failure talk. Time Line and situation – walk through it.

c) **Phobia Cure**: for failure situations.

d) **Discussion**: of questions & more Orientation. Swish for failure situation.

3. Distress was the target of the third workshop, and the attempt is made to reduce the amount of felt distress (affect) and distress proneness – on the assumption that this will reduce distress intolerance. Methods for each section of the day were

a) **Orientation to Distress**: Stress/Anxiety Management orientation and physiological self-regulation methods.

b) **RET and Assertive Training**: as means to deal with felt distress/discomfort. Effort here to reduce distress.

c) **Time Line**: for a significant emotional experience. Rapid Phobia Method to deal with emotional experience.

d) **Relaxation & Desensitization**: Relaxation training, and start-up systematic desensitization (with and without eye tracking) for distress situations. Assertive training.

4. Sensitivity was the target of the fourth workshop, and the attempt is made to reduce empathy or sensitivity to others – based on the assumption that this will reduce sensitivity intolerance. Methods for each section of the day were

a) **Orientation to Empathic Sensitivity**: *"Must*erbation" (as Ellis would call it) and beliefs derived from attitudes and actions of adults. It is impossible to hurt another person emotionally by what you do. The error of anger.

b) **Concept Formation & Reframing**: Abstraction training and how concepts/ideas are formed. How do you make yourself feel you have hurt another person? Swish to neutralize sensitizing situations (hurt vs. no hurt).

    c) **Time-Line & Resources**: Time-Line and walk through some situations of being told you hurt another, this time with brought back resources.

    d) **Relaxation & Desensitization**: Relaxation and use of the "fast phobia" movie method for "you hurt me."

5. Obsessive Rumination was the target of the fifth workshop,[9] and the attempt is made to reduce introspection and worries – on the assumption that this will reduce the associated closeness assumption for each section of the day were

    a) **Orientation to Thought Pressure**: Introversion and verbal mediation of experience. How do you make yourself think and worry? Uncertainty intolerance. Anger inhibition. Self-restraint and rage. Assertive training.

    b) **Activity & Zen**: The reciprocal inhibition of thought and action. Thought as anticipation (fear) or reminiscence (depression). Living in the present. Zen principles.

    c) **Meditation & Thought Regulation**: All thought is useless. Meditation orientation and practice.

    d) **Boredom & Enjoyment**: Habits of long intervals of concentration – boredom. Short-interval timetabling. How to enjoy life and finding "good" things.

6. Discipline was the target of the sixth workshop, and the attempt is made to reduce (experienced) external discipline and increase

---

[9] One previously unmentioned aspect of this treatment program involved the desire to utilize a variety of treatment methodologies. Targeting the obsessive rumination, instead of sensitivity to either closeness or rejection, allowed us to test a variety of cognitive methods that we had not previously deployed. In practice, that turned out to be a mistake, since it did not have the desired affect on Factor 5, Hypersensitivity to and rejection of Closeness.

freedom – assuming that this will reduce discipline intolerance. Methods for each section of the day were:

a) **Orientation to Discipline**: Attitudes toward punishment as reward and as rejection. The evidence you were loved. Evidences of love. Purposes of discipline. How do you make yourself feel rebellious?
b) **Cognitive Therapy & RET**: Common mistakes of thinking. Correcting self-talk. Reframing others' actions.
c) **Relaxation & Swish**: Relaxation training. Swish for restrictions- discipline/freedom images.
d) **Desensitization**: Desensitization for discipline events.

Preparing to Test the Validity of the Postulated
Psychodynamics of the STFB

Is there any validity in these formulations? Obviously, our conjectures about how all of this works are speculative. However, although ordered to suit a kind of psychological view of development, the various steps in the developmental sequences offered are taken fairly directly from the contents of the items endorsed by offenders who scored in the upper range of each of the factors. Of course, the real question of importance in such formulations lies in their value in directing the prevention and treatment of the thinking, feelings and behaviours implied in each of the criminality factors, and in the eventual determination of the effects, if any, of interventions derived either to prevent or to reduce the criminal behaviours attributable to these cognitive-affective components of criminality.

Although we had frequently considered offenders to have characteristics similar to the "neurotic" patients with whom we had worked during the early parts of our careers, except that offenders tended to externalize (i.e., to act out their internal conflicts) rather than internalize (i.e., to hold their distress within), we had not really thought very much about how that difference came about. But what if offenders merely had reached the point at which they felt the distress of each factor's dynamics too poignantly, and simply could not tolerate the negative experiences that ensued? Or what if the pressures to which they had been subjected were imposed at a developmental stage more appropriate to acting out than to acceptance of the neurotic distress? – an idea which harks back to the concept of the "neurotic character disorder" and the work of early researchers in the field of delinquency.

Gradually, the idea that the angry, distress-rejecting reactions common to the psychodynamics postulated to underlie each of the STFB factors represented an intolerable "burden" that the offender was not about to bear became the focus around which each of our treatment programs was organized; and we began to consider the task of treatment as involving an attempt to decrease the pressure of the underlying distress implied in each factor's dynamics, rather than seeking to enhance or increase the apparent deficiencies implied by the offender's defensive acting out behaviours. For example, to the extent that criminal behaviour is motivated by a sensitivity to (and, hence, a rejection of) feelings of guilt, perhaps that sensitivity is the problem which should be addressed. If sensitivity to failure is the issue, perhaps that is what needs to be addressed, and so on.

Finding a Suitable Treatment Modality

Just how might this treatment be done? Obviously, if an attempt was to be made to evaluate any treatment undertaken and at the same time to evaluate the modifiability of the STFB factors, it would require that (1) a large number of offenders be treated, (2) each in more-or-less the same way, and (3) in relatively short intervals of time. The concept of the treatment workshop seemed to provide one way in which that might be accomplished.

Even though the Ontario Correctional Institute was viewed as the "flagship" correctional treatment centre in Ontario, it had been provided with clinical resources at less than one-quarter of the level

called for in hospital standards for a treatment centre of its size –
Correctional Services administrators tend to think of staffing levels
in terms of what is needed for the average jail. As a result, for some
years, psychology staff at the OCI had been exploring the upper
limits in size of a treatment group that might be conducted without
loss of therapeutic benefits. The present authors had begun with 20
inmate participants, increased to 25, increased to 35, increased to
50 and, finally, increased to 75 – the largest number that could be
accommodated in the largest group room to which they had access.

Each successively larger group was administered a battery of
monitoring tests before and after treatment to measure therapeutic
changes, if any, which took place. The results obtained in these
"large-group treatment workshops" had proven to be most
auspicious. In treatment program after treatment program, far from
finding a "ceiling effect" above which treatment effects could not be
demonstrated, it was observed that as group size was increased, so
did measurable amounts of therapeutic benefit to the average inmate
subject (Quirk and Reynolds, 1991), as if some sort of mobilizing
effect (or contagion) increases with group size. Eventually, we
concluded that satisfactory treatment effects could theoretically be
accomplished in groups of any size that could be accommodated in a
suitably appointed room – a conclusion that would not be inconsistent
with the large-group results that have been achieved by, for example,
the commercially-available Smokenders program. Moreover, within
limits, the duration of a treatment program could apparently be
extended to fill an entire working day. The limits appeared to bear
upon subjects' attention spans. That is, a day-long program could
be run without loss of therapeutic effects as long as ample provision
was made for "breaks," as long as no session lasted more than an
hour or so, and as long as ample provision was made to capture
and maintain both attention and motivation in the participants.
These requirements, however, turned out to be little more than quite
manageable technical issues.

The Large-Group Treatment of Criminality

Since inmates are admitted to the OCI, and from the intake unit to the living units, on the basis of bed availability, and since they are released from the living units upon the completion of their sentences, the assumption was made that assigning inmates to treatment groups according to their discharge dates would provide a satisfactory basis for randomization of group assignment. Thus, on a particular day, the inmates who were residing at the OCI were listed in order according to their discharge dates – after first having excluded those half dozen inmates identified by their case management staff as possessing too little by way of criminalistic traits to warrant their inclusion in a criminality treatment program – and were assigned sequentially to either a treatment or a control group. Although neither of two sets of Control Group subjects were invited to attend (and none of the Control Group subjects did attend) any of the STFB-related treatment programs, they did participate in other regular treatment programs throughout their incarceration, like all of the other inmates at the OCI.[10]

The following table shows how subjects were assigned to the criminality treatment programs and their control groups:

STFB or Other TARGET								
Group Assignment (sequentially by release date)	Relapse Prevention ("Control")	STFB Factor 1	STFB Factor 2	STFB Factor 3	STFB Factor 4	STFB Factor 5	STFB Factor 6	Values
Control Group 1	T							
Trx Workshop 1		T						
Trx Workshop 2			T					

---

[10] An effort was made by the correctional staff and the various other professions to create a therapeutic environment on each of the living units. In addition, Psychology, social work, education, and chaplaincy staff each had their own treatment interests and programs that they felt were important approaches to helping the same inmates in which we were interested. That became a problem when this workshop program proved it to be effective, since everyone else ignored this treatment approach in favour of continuing to pursue their own interests.

Trx Workshop 3			T				
Trx Workshop 4				T			
Trx Workshop 5					T		
Trx Workshop 6						T	
Trx Group 1, 3, 5	T		T		T		
Trx Group 2, 4, 6		T		T		T	
Trx Group 1 to 6	T	T	T	T	T	T	
Trx Group 1 to 6 plus Values *	T	T	T	T	T	T	T
Control Group 2							

* Because of the possible confounding effect of the Values workshops, the data from this group are not considered in this paper.

Day-long programs were designed to address the motivations presumed to underlie each of the six criminal thinking factors, and presented in large-group treatment workshop format; and changes in factor scale scores from pre- to post-treatment were examined to determine the extent to which we were successful in modifying criminal thinking.

The six separate treatment-of-criminal-thinking workshop program plans (each one addressing a different criminal thinking factor) were as follows: [11]

1. **Guilt** was the target of the first workshop, and the attempt was made to reduce the amount of guilt feeling and guilt proneness – on the assumption that this would have the effect of reducing guilt intolerance.
2. **Failure** was the target of the second workshop, and the attempt was made to reduce the amount of failure feeling and failure proneness – on the assumption that this would have the effect of reducing failure intolerance.
3. **Distress** was the target of the third workshop, and the attempt was made to reduce the amount of felt distress (affect) and distress

---

[11]   A reasonably extensive description of some of the treatment components used in these workshops is given in Appendix C.

proneness – on the assumption that this would reduce distress intolerance.

4. **Sensitivity** was the target of the fourth workshop, and the attempt was made to reduce sensitivity to others – based on the assumption that this would reduce sensitivity intolerance.

5. **Obsessive Rumination** was the target of the fifth workshop, and the attempt was made to reduce introspection and worries – on the assumption that this would reduce the associated closeness intolerance.

6. **Discipline** was the target of the sixth workshop, and the attempt was made to reduce the subjective experience of external discipline and to increase the subjective experience of freedom – on the assumption that this would reduce discipline intolerance.

Immediate Effects of the Criminality Treatment Workshops:

Examination of change in STFB Total score – our main measure of criminality – as a function of total hours attended at criminality treatments found that a decrease in criminality (as measured by the STFB) was directly related to the total number of hours of treatment received.

Given the brief time allowed for each treatment program – little more than four hours – it was decided that, in analyses involving comparisons between the Treatment and Control groups, an inmate would have to have attended any given treatment workshop for at least three of the four approximately-hour-long segments of each workshop (i.e., for at least 3 hours) to be included in the treatment group. Thus, groups were assembled containing only those inmates who had attended either for at least 3 hours (the treatment groups) or for 0 hours (the Control group) for each treatment program; and Treatment and Control groups were compared using between-groups t-tests.

Change in STFB Total Score As A Function of
Total Workshop Attendance Hours

Hours Attended	0	1-6	7-12	13-18	19-24
N	68	83	29	6	14
Total Change	1.27	1.27	3.62	4.16	4.77

Next, residual gains scores were calculated to represent pre- to post-test changes on the six STFB factors and on the STFB Total, Neutral and Undesirable scales, and change scores were examined for each STFB factor for each workshop, to see if the treatments chosen for inclusion in each workshop were appropriately selected and/or *differentially* effective.

Change in STFB Factor Scores as a Function
of Criminality Treatment Provided[12]

STFB Factor Treatments	N	Factor 1	Factor 2	Factor 3	Factor 4	Factor 5	Factor 6
Change in Targeted Treatment	N's Vary	0.88	1.12	0.84	1.02	0.78	1.14
2-tailed Statistical Significance[13]		**0.00**	**0.00**	**0.00**	**0.00**	**0.03**	**0.00**

---

[12]   Correlations may range from -1.00 (a perfect negative correlation, in which one score goes up while the other goes down) to 1.00 (in which both scores go either up or down together).

The following table presents the probabilities that there is no relationship (the so-called "null hypothesis") between each treatment and its effect on each of the STFB factor scale scores. Those inmate subjects who received 3-4 hours of their particular criminality treatment workshops showed significant changes in targeted STFB factor scale scores from pre- to post-treatment for five of the six workshops. The exception was the workshop that we intended to reduce the score on STFB Factor 5 – and we will return to that result shortly since the failure of this treatment workshop to effect changes in its targetted STFB factor turned out to be more apparent than real.

In order to emphasize the rather arresting pattern of results obtained in these analyses, significant probabilities are highlighted.

---

[13] When comparing the effect of treatment on groups of subjects, statistical significance refers to the probability that observed differences between the treatment and control groups is not just due to sampling error. Typically, in significance testing, these probabilities (or "p" values) are considered to be significant if p is equal to or less than 0.05 ($p \leq 0.05$). If $p \leq 0.05$, there is no more than one chance in twenty that the observed difference between the groups being compared was not indicative that a similar difference would be observed in the larger population from which the groups were drawn. A p value of 0.10 might be acceptable if no prediction is made concerning the direction of difference between the groups being compared (a two-tailed test of significance) – that is, those comparisons in which measures of treatment effects were not hypothesized to be changed in a given direction by the particular treatment, i.e., Workshop 1 on Factors 2 through 6, Workshop 2 on Factor 1 and Factors 3 through 6, etc.).

In these tables, N refers to number of subjects receiving the treatment(s). For the sake of clarity, N's (number of subjects) given in each table are for the targeted factor comparison. N's for other comparisons often differed slightly.

Summary of Probabilities of Effects of Treatment
Workshops 1 to 6 (independent variables) on
STFB Factors 1 to 6 (dependent variables)

STFB Factor Change by Tx Workshop	Factor 1	Factor 2	Factor 3	Factor 4	Factor 5	Factor 6
Treatment 1	**.05**	.18	**.07**	.11	.68	**.04**
Treatment 2	.13	**.00**	.18	.30	.28	**.00**
Treatment 3	.60	.35	**.10**	.42	.99	.13
Treatment 4	.34	**.01**	.29	**.07**	.38	**.00**
Treatment 5	.12	.09	.39	.44	.42	.62
Treatment 6	**.08**	**.06**	.36	.39	.51	**.00**

These treatment results indicate that at least reasonably appropriate treatments were selected and that, to a considerable extent, "differential treatment" was accomplished. That is, as a general rule, the treatments were generally successful in effecting change in the criminality factors that they targeted, and occasionally effective in changing other criminality factors as well.

To reiterate, with the exception of the fifth workshop, which we had hoped would modify Factor 5, subjects who participated in three or more hours of any of the specific criminality treatments showed a significant decrease in the STFB factor targeted by that treatment, compared to control group subjects who participated in a "relapse prevention" workshop.

Change in STFB Factor Scores as a Function
of Relapse Prevention Only

STFB Factor by Relapse Prevention Workshop	N	Factor 1	Factor 2	Factor 3	Factor 4	Factor 5	Factor 6
Relapse Prevention Only	18	0.60	0.39	− 0.22	0.87	0.69	0.12
2-tail Sig		0.18	0.21	0.63	0.17	**0.03**	0.79

However, Control group subjects who participated in three or more hours of a "Relapse Prevention" workshop (and none of the criminality treatment workshops) showed a significant decrease in STFB Factor 5 (and no change in any of the other STFB factors), which is why the difference obtained between treatment and control groups for Factor 5 was not statistically significant; and control subjects who received no treatment workshop hours at all showed no change in any of the STFB factors at all.

Apparently the workshop that we intended to modify STFB Factor 5 effected changes in Factor 5, and the initial apparent failure of this workshop to affect its targeted STFB factor can be attributed to the fact that Factor 5 was also modified by the Relapse Prevention program that was (1) used in this study as a "control" treatment and (2) received by some of the no-criminality-treatment control subjects – which, of course, blunted the statistical test comparing the experimental and control group subjects.

For comparison purposes, change in STFB Factor Scores was also examined for the group that received none of these treatment workshops. Interestingly, there *was* a significant change in Factor 6 – Hypersensitivity To And Rejection Of Discipline – in that no-treatment-workshop group, but in the wrong direction!

Change in STFB Factor Scores With No
Treatment Workshops At All

	N	Change Factor 1	Change Factor 2	Change Factor 3	Change Factor 4	Change Factor 5	Change Factor 6
STFB Factor Change by No Workshop At All	18	0.12	− 0.22	0.48	0.31	0.35	− 0.47
2-tail Sig		0.73	0.44	0.14	0.38	0.33	**0.08**

Measuring the Long-Term Effects of Correctional Treatment

The fact that treatments based on the psychodynamics postulated to underlie and "drive" each of the aspects of criminality measured by the STFB resulted in significant changes on each of their targeted factors might be said to provide some support for the predictive validity of the STFB. However, as we all know, the ultimate test of the effectiveness of correctional treatment resides in its ability to influence recidivism rates and, for that, it was necessary to await the release and subsequent re-offence or non-offence of those inmates who participated in this study (which required that we wait two years post-release before doing follow-up on the inmates who participated in the study). That two-year waiting period being fulfilled, the results are now in. Before we get to them, however, it is necessary to say a few words about recidivism.

In most correctional outcome evaluation work, program effectiveness is determined by differential recidivism rates for treated and untreated offenders. Too frequently, recidivism has been expressed as a dichotomous variable established by the presence or absence of specific outcome criteria such as further arrests, further convictions or further incarcerations. Researchers have long recognized the inadequacies of such all-or-none measures and of the recidivism rates derived from them (Maltz, 1984). The usual criticism is that the dichotomous nature of the recidivism variable ignores a substantial amount of relevant information about the recidivistic event, which reduces the ability of researchers to discriminate among groups and lowers the likelihood of being able to document varying degrees of impact of correctional programs on individual offender's post-release performance.

It has been suggested that improved discrimination might be achieved by examining the distribution of survival times, represented by time on the street before recidivism – a sort of "resistance to recidivism" measure of outcome, as it were – and we have used this measure as one of our outcome criteria. Another measure that we considered was the Sellin & Wolfgang (1964) Offence Seriousness Index, which has been investigated extensively (Blumstein, 1974; Bridges & Lisagor, 1975; Figlio, 1975; Gottfredson, Young & Laufer, 1980; Hindelang, 1974; Kelly & Winslow, 1973; Lesieur & Lehman, 1975; Rose, 1966; Wagner & Pease, 1978; Walker, 1978; Wellford & Wiatrowski, 1975) and replicated internationally (Akman & Normandeau, 1968; Hsu, 1973; Normandeau, 1966; Rossi, Waite, Bose & Berk, 1974; Velez-Diaz & Megargee, 1971) and which has gained wide recognition as an index of crime in society. It is probably the most sophisticated method available for measuring offence seriousness, and its use of behaviour descriptions of criminalistic events means that, in principle, transferral across jurisdictions should be possible.

Unfortunately, its utility for correctional treatment research purposes is limited, at least in Ontario, by the difficulty of transforming the categories used in the prison records available to us into the behavioural descriptions that the Offence Seriousness Index uses as its scoring criteria. That is, as a general rule, the only records available to us and, we suspect, to most correctional researchers, tend to contain only category of offence, number of counts, and the sentence imposed. And even if police occurrence reports are available, they rarely contain the kind of detail needed to score offenses on the Offence Seriousness Index. Thus, for most program evaluation research, the usefulness and accuracy of this scale in measuring offence seriousness is seriously limited by the descriptive information in the records available.

However, this paper is not intended to be about the Offense Seriousness Index or its next generation development, The National Survey of Crime Severity (Wolfgang, Figlio, Tracy & Singer, 1985). Suffice it to say that a comparison between the National Survey of Crime Severity and the simple and readily available criterion of Offence Seriousness, as indicated by length of sentence imposed, found the latter measure to be a much better criterion of recidivism, and that is the measure that was used in this study.

Effect of the Criminality Treatment Workshops on Recidivism

Examination of two year post release records of the subjects included in this study found significant relationships, as indicated by the correlations between the number of treatment workshops attended and two separate indicators of recidivism (time on the street, i.e., until re-offence) and severity of re-offence. That is, the statistic being examined for significance is the correlation between the two variables, the number of treatment workshops attended and three separate indicators of recidivism, and significance was achieved for two of the three measures of recidivism.

Recidivism as a Function of Treatment Workshops Attended

	Conviction or Not	Time on the Street	Seriousness of Offence
Number of Treatment Workshops Attended[1]	− 0.10	0.14	− 0.14
Significance[2]	p = .15	**p = .03**	**p = .04**

[1] Controlling for attendance at the "Control" workshop.
[2] Two-tailed

In fact, almost half of the subjects who received no treatment workshops at all recidivated, as might have been expected, while *none* of the subjects who were assigned to and participated in three or more of the criminality treatment workshops recidivated within the two year post release follow-up period!

In addition, significant relationships were found between changes in STFB scores as a result of treatment and all three of our indicators of recidivism (re-conviction, time on the street, and severity of re-offence).

Recidivism as a Function of Change in STFB [14]

Residual Gain Scores	Conviction or Not	Time on the Street	Seriousness of Offence
Factor 1	0.15	− 0.15	0.10
Factor 2	0.08	− 0.09	0.04
Factor 3	0.03	0.02	− 0.09
Factor 4	0.09	− 0.08	0.10
Factor 5	0.18 *	− 0.18 *	0.15 *
Factor 6	0.22 **	− 0.17 *	0.12
STFB Total	0.19 *	− 0.16 *	0.09
STFB Neutral	0.17 *	− 0.12	0.19 *
STFB Undesirable	0.17 *	− 0.19 *	0.10

[1] Controlling for Age
[2] * $p < 0.05$ (two-tailed) ** $p < 0.01$ (two-tailed)

It had been thought that final STFB scores would also be related to recidivism, but here the relationship is somewhat less robust – the only statistically significant relationships were between time on the street and the final (absolute rather than change) scores on (1) Factor

[14] Interestingly, change in STFB Factor 5 was the only change score that was significantly related to all three of our recidivism measures.

6 (Hypersensitivity to and Rejection of Discipline) and (2) the STFB
Social Undesirability scale.

Recidivism as a Function of Post-Treatment STFB Scores [1]

Post-Treatment STFB Scores	Conviction or Not	Time on the Street	Seriousness of Offence
Factor 1	0.07	− 0.06	0.00
Factor 2	0.07	− 0.04	0.02
Factor 3	− 0.01	0.02	− 0.09
Factor 4	− 0.03	0.00	0.02
Factor 5	− 0.04	0.03	− 0.06
Factor 6	0.10	**− 0.11**	0.09
STFB Total	0.03	− 0.03	− 0.01
STFB Neutral	− 0.00	0.06	0.01
STFB Undesirable	0.08	**− 0.11**	0.05

[1] Controlling for Age.

Summary and Conclusions

In summary, the Survey of Thoughts, Feelings and Behaviours
(STFB) has been shown to be a useful measure of criminality. It
provides meaningful, if unexpected, views of the roots of criminality.
Its scores have been shown to be modifiable by treatment methods
that are both brief and capable of being delivered in cost-effective
large-group format; and both the amount of treatment provided and
the extent to which STFB scores are modified by these treatment
workshops have been shown to be related to two-year-post-release
recidivism. That is, the treatment workshops both lowered STFB
criminality scores and resulted in lower recidivism rates, as measured
by whether or not subjects re-offended, time on the street until re-
offence, and seriousness of re-offence in the two years post-release.

Given the scant amount of treatment provided, it is amazing that any effect at all was still measurable at two years post-release. And since even the token amount of treatment provided in this study did, in fact, lower recidivism, this particular approach to thinking about, measuring, and treating criminality would seem to warrant further investigation and application.

Addendum

In the interest of the continuing pursuit of truth – which is what science is all about – we wondered whether the same efficacious six factor solution would have emerged if we had been examining a different sample of subjects, rather than those who had been included in this particular study. Appendix D details the results of that investigation.

Appendix A

SURVEY OF THOUGHTS, FEELINGS AND BEHAVIOURS

Name:_____

Age:_____ Sex:_____

INSTRUCTIONS:

This inventory consists of numbered statements.

Read each statement and decide whether in your opinion it is TRUE or FALSE. Becauseeveryone has a right to his or her own opinion, there are no "right" or "wrong" answers.

You are to mark your answers on the questionnaire, in the place provided.

If a statement is TRUE or MOSTLY TRUE in your opinion, place a mark on the line in The column headed T (see A at the right).

If a statement is FALSE or NOT USUALLY TRUE in your opinion, place a mark on the line in the column headed F (see B at the right).

Please try to give a response to every statement.

Example: Section of the questionnaire correctly marked.

	T	F
A	__ X __	_____
B	_____	__ X __

Make your marks heavy and black. Erase completely any answer you wish to change.

Now open the booklet and go ahead.

SURVEY OF THOUGHTS, FEELINGS AND BEHAVIOURS

T   F

___ ___ 1. I only like activities that are exciting.

___ ___ 2. People are more likely to say that I am a responsible person than that I am mature.

___ ___ 3. I sometimes let fear stand in the way of doing what I want to do.

___ ___ 4. I like most people more than I like animals.

___ ___ 5. When I make a decision I go by how I feel at the time.

___ ___ 6. The risks involved in a life of crime would be enough to keep me from trying it.

___ ___ 7. The only time I care about is right now.

___ ___ 8. I trust others and I expect them to trust me.

___ ___ 9. I have never felt that I was a "nothing".

___ ___ 10. I can't stand it when people get in the way of what I want.

___ ___ 11. I would get a thrill out of seeing a newspaper story about something illegal that I had done and gotten away with.

___ ___ 12. I have never felt that I was getting a raw deal from life.

___ ___ 13. Church attendance doesn't tell you very much about whether or not a person is religious.

___ ___ 14. I feel that I am not the same as everybody else.

___ ___ 15. Since no two situations are the same, how can I be expected to learn from my mistakes.

___ ___ 16. When I'm thinking about doing something that I know is wrong, I will sometimes hear voices telling me not to do it.

___ ___ 17. It doesn't matter how you do it, just so long as you come out on top.

___ ___ 18. I don't feel any need to keep people from getting too close to me.

___ ___ 19. I was not interested in most of the subjects that I took at school.

___ ___ 20. I have had more than my share of hard times.

___ ___ 21. I live every day as if it were my last.

___ ___ 22. Being dependent on others is not a sign of weakness.

_____ _____ 23. Since everyone breaks the law, it isn't fair that only some people get punished for it.

_____ _____ 24. If you don't destroy fear, it will destroy you.

_____ _____ 25. I always think things through carefully before making an important decision.

_____ _____ 26. Just because you help people in need doesn't mean that you are a good person.

_____ _____ 27. Even if I really wanted to do something, my fears could keep me from doing it.

_____ _____ 28. There is no point in forcing yourself to do a job that you don't want to do.

_____ _____ 29. I have never heard voices telling me to behave myself.

_____ _____ 30. The main difference between criminals and other people is that the criminals have been caught.

_____ _____ 31. There is no good reason for most of the things that I have done.

_____ _____ 32. I often feel that people can see right through me.

_____ _____ 33. I could not hate someone one minute and love him or her the next.

_____ _____ 34. I often get into trouble for not paying bills, tickets, etc.

_____ _____ 35. I have sometimes been talked into "easy money" schemes.

_____ _____ 36. I have rarely been a victim of the system.

_____ _____ 37. My life is planned well in advance.

_____ _____ 38. I am not interested in other people's problems.

_____ _____ 39. I can allow myself to fail.

_____ _____ 40. When I am in a relationship, I often feel as if I own the other person.

_____ _____ 41. Just the thought of going to prison would be enough to keep me on the straight and narrow.

_____ _____ 42. Not everyone has things that they are afraid of.

_____ _____ 43. Before I take on a job, I want to know that it will pay me what I am worth.

_____ _____ 44. I would not find it hard to imagine what hell is really like.

_____ _____ 45. Chairs are not just for sitting on.

_____ _____ 46. It is only fair that criminals get sent to jail.

_____ _____ 47. I am really good at sex.

_____ _____ 48. I am not easily talked into "get rich quick" schemes.

_____ _____ 49. I have never felt that I was different from everybody else.

_____ _____ 50. In this world, you say what you must to get what you want.

___ ___	51.	Even if I don't want to do something, I can't just ignore what I have been told to do.
___ ___	52.	Before making a decision, I want to know how it will affect other people.
___ ___	53.	The seriousness of an assault doesn't just depend on the amount of physical damage that is done.
___ ___	54.	I have often been late for work.
___ ___	55.	I do not get fed up very easily.
___ ___	56.	I decided at an early age that I would have to "go it alone."
___ ___	57.	Crime is not a job just like any other kind of job.
___ ___	58.	In my books, anyone who is kind to animals is a good person.
___ ___	59.	When I really want to do something, my conscience goes right out the window.
___ ___	60.	I don't intend to be much better than I am.
___ ___	61.	If I became afraid while doing something wrong, the fear would not add to my enjoyment of it.
___ ___	62.	When my mind is made up, nothing can change it.
___ ___	63.	I prefer a life that is not too exciting.
___ ___	64.	All of the experts that I have met know more than I do.
___ ___	65.	I find it fairly easy to stay away from trouble.
___ ___	66.	Just before doing something forbidden, I often find myself becoming excited.
___ ___	67.	I worry about any harm that I do to others, even when I know that their insurance will take care of it.
___ ___	68.	No matter how severe the penalty, people will do what they want to do anyway.
___ ___	69.	If I am not on top then I am on the bottom.
___ ___	70.	I have never gotten into serious fights over small things.
___ ___	71.	It is hard for me to turn down an invitation to a party.
___ ___	72.	I get really mad whenever I see anyone strike a child.
___ ___	73.	I can admit to being afraid.
___ ___	74.	I rarely think about doing anything that is against the law.
___ ___	75.	As a teenager, I was not very active sexually.
___ ___	76.	I learned early in life that it is usually best to tell the truth.
___ ___	77.	I don't like to reveal my plans for the future in case people might try to interfere with them.
___ ___	78.	If it weren't for other people things would have turned out better for me.

____ ____ 79. It is usually a mistake to live just for today.

____ ____ 80. I usually get what I want.

____ ____ 81. I have been let down so often that I find it hard to let myself trust anyone.

____ ____ 82. The years I spent in school were not wasted.

____ ____ 83. I can usually tell what a person is like within minutes of meeting him or her.

____ ____ 84. I do whatever I want to do when there is little risk of getting caught.

____ ____ 85. I never start a job until I feel sure that everything is going to go the way that I want it to go.

____ ____ 86. It is foolish to put yourself in the position where you have to depend on other people.

____ ____ 87. If I became afraid when doing something wrong, it would just remind me to be more careful.

____ ____ 88. Few people get hurt unless they have been asking for it.

____ ____ 89. If I made a lot of money through crime, I wouldn't care how I spent it, just so long as I had a good time.

____ ____ 90. I would not get much excitement out of seeing how much I could get away with.

____ ____ 91. I usually do what my conscience tells me to do.

____ ____ 92. I generally feel understood.

____ ____ 93. The first thing that I notice when I enter a store is the location of the cash register.

____ ____ 94. If I wanted to do something badly enough, I could easily rid myself of any fears I might have about doing it.

____ ____ 95. I would not find it exciting to put one over on the police.

____ ____ 96. If I made some money through crime, I would be more likely to save it than to spend it.

____ ____ 97. Punishment doesn't have much effect on me.

____ ____ 98. Alcohol cannot be blamed for very much of the crime in society.

____ ____ 99. There would be less crime if more criminals were sent to prison.

____ ____ 100. It doesn't bother me to talk about my feelings.

STFB ANSWER SHEET

Name:_____

Age:_____ Sex:_____

Education:_____

Please place a mark on the appropriate line, to indicate whether, in your opinion, the item is Mainly True or Mainly False.

	T	F		T	F		T	F		T	F		T	F
1.	—	—	21.	—	—	41.	—	—	61.	—	—	81.	—	—
2.	—	—	22.	—	—	42.	—	—	62.	—	—	82.	—	—
3.	—	—	23.	—	—	43.	—	—	63.	—	—	83.	—	—
4.	—	—	24.	—	—	44.	—	—	64.	—	—	84.	—	—
5.	—	—	25.	—	—	45.	—	—	65.	—	—	85.	—	—
6.	—	—	26.	—	—	46.	—	—	66.	—	—	86.	—	—
7.	—	—	27.	—	—	47.	—	—	67.	—	—	87.	—	—
8.	—	—	28.	—	—	48.	—	—	68.	—	—	88.	—	—
9.	—	—	29.	—	—	49.	—	—	69.	—	—	89.	—	—
10.	—	—	30.	—	—	50.	—	—	70.	—	—	90.	—	—

	T	F		T	F		T	F		T	F		T	F
11.	—	—	31.	—	—	51.	—	—	71.	—	—	91.	—	—
12.	—	—	32.	—	—	52.	—	—	72.	—	—	92.	—	—
13.	—	—	33.	—	—	53.	—	—	73.	—	—	93.	—	—
14.	—	—	34.	—	—	54.	—	—	74.	—	—	94.	—	—
15.	—	—	35.	—	—	55.	—	—	75.	—	—	95.	—	—
16.	—	—	36.	—	—	56.	—	—	76.	—	—	96.	—	—
17.	—	—	37.	—	—	57.	—	—	77.	—	—	97.	—	—
18.	—	—	38.	—	—	58.	—	—	78.	—	—	98.	—	—
19.	—	—	39.	—	—	59.	—	—	79.	—	—	99.	—	—
20.	—	—	40.	—	—	60.	—	—	80.	—	—	100.	—	—

STFB SCORING

Name:_____

Score the STFB according to the following chart.

	T	F		T	F		T	F		T	F		T	F
1.	1	0	21.	1	0	41.	0	1	61.	0	1	81.	1	0
2.	0	1	22.	0	1	42.	1	0	62.	1	0	82.	0	1
3.	0	1	23.	1	0	43.	1	0	63.	0	1	83.	1	0
4.	0	1	24.	1	0	44.	1	0	64.	0	1	84.	1	0
5.	1	0	25.	0	1	45.	0	1	65.	0	1	85.	1	0
6.	0	1	26.	0	1	46.	0	1	66.	1	0	86.	1	0
7.	0	1	27.	0	1	47.	0	1	67.	1	0	87.	1	0
8.	0	1	28.	1	0	48.	0	1	68.	1	0	88.	1	0
9.	0	1	29.	1	0	49.	1	0	69.	1	0	89.	1	0
10.	1	0	30.	1	0	50.	1	0	70.	1	0	90.	0	1

	T	F		T	F		T	F		T	F		T	F
11.	1	0	31.	1	0	51.	0	1	71.	1	0	91.	0	1
12.	0	1	32.	1	0	52.	0	1	72.	1	0	92.	0	1
13.	0	1	33.	0	1	53.	0	1	73.	0	1	93.	1	0
14.	0	1	34.	1	0	54.	1	0	74.	0	1	94.	1	0
15.	1	0	35.	1	0	55.			75.	0	1	95.	0	1
16.			36.	0	1	56.	1	0	76.	0	1	96.	0	1
17.	1	0	37.	0	1	57.	0	1	77.	1	0	97.	1	0
18.	0	1	38.	1	0	58.	1	0	78.	1	0	98.	0	1
19.	1	0	39.			59.	1	0	79.	0	1	99.	0	1
20.	1	0	40.	1	0	60.	0	1	80.	0	1	100.	0	1

Alternatively, if you code each True response as 1 and each False response as 2, use the following recoding procedure to calculate the value of each item and the scales derived from them.

STFB RECODING PROCEDURE

Recode x1, x5, x7, x10, x11, x15, x17, x19, x20, x21, x23, x24, x28, x29, x30, x31, x32, x34, x35, x38, x40, x42, x43, x44, x47, x49, x50, x54, x56, x58, x59, x62, x66, x68, x69, x71, x72, x77, x78, x81, x83, x84, x85, x86, x87, x88, x89, x93, x94, x97 (0=0) (1=1) (2=0).

Recode x2, x3, x4, x6, x8, x9, x12, x13, x14, x16, x18, x22, x25, x26, x27, x33, x36, x37, x39, x41, x45, x46, x48, x51, x52, x53, x55, x57, x60, x61, x63, x64, x65, x67, x70, x73, x74, x75, x76, x79, x80, x82, x90, x91, x92, x95, x96, x98, x99, x100 (0=0) (1=0) (2=1).

CALCULATION OF STFB SCALE SCORES

Compute s1 = mean (x16, x29)

Compute s2 = mean. (x59, x91)

Compute s3 = mean (x27, x94)

Compute s4 = mean (x61, x87)

Compute s5 = mean (x6, x84)

Compute s6 = mean (x66, x90)

Compute s7 = mean (x38, x52)

Compute s8 = mean (x41, x97)

Compute s26 = mean (x42, x73)

Compute s27 = mean (x7, x37)

Compute s28 = mean (x21, x79)

Compute s29 = mean (x65, x71)

Compute s30 = mean (x89, x96)

Compute s31 = mean (x15, x45)

Compute s32 = mean (x17, x53)

Compute s33 = mean (x31, x98)

Compute s9 = mean (x23, x46)

Compute s10 = mean (x13, x44)

Compute s11 = mean (x12, x20)

Compute s12 = mean (x36, x78)

Compute s13 = mean (x18, x56)

Compute s14 = mean (x51, x62)

Compute s15 = mean (x39, x85)

Compute s16 = mean (x19, x82)

Compute s17 = mean (x28, x55)

Compute s18 = mean (x43, x64)

Compute s19 = mean (x47, x75)

Compute s20 = mean (x1, x63)

Compute s21 = mean (x2, x54)

Compute s22 = mean x50, x76)

Compute s23 = mean (x8, x81)

Compute s24 = mean (x9, x32)

Compute s25 = mean (x77, x100)

Compute s34 = mean (x14, x49)

Compute s35 = mean (x33, x69)

Compute s36 = mean (x22, x86)

Compute s37 = mean (x4, x72)

Compute s38 = mean (x83, x92)

Compute s39 = mean (x40, x80)

Compute s40 = mean (x67, x88)

Compute s41 = mean (x26, x58)

Compute s42 = mean (x11, x95)

Compute s43 = mean (x74, x93)

Compute s44 = mean (x3, x24)

Compute s45 = mean (x35, x48)

Compute s46 = mean (x34, x60)

Compute s47 = mean (x5, x25)

Compute s49 = mean (x10, x70)

Compute s49 = mean (x68, x99)

Compute s50 = mean (x30, x57)

Compute f1 = mean (s1, s2, s3, s4, s5, s6, s7, s8, s9, s10) x 10

Compute f2 = mean (s11, s12, s13, s14, s15, s16, s17, s18, s19, s20, s21) x 10

Compute f3 = mean (s22, s23, s24, s25, s26, s27, s28, s29, s30) x 10

Compute f4 = mean (s31, s32, s33, s34) x 10

Compute f5 = mean (s35, s36, s37, s38, s39, s40, s41, s42, s43) x 10

Compute f6 = mean (s44, s45, s46, s47, s48, s49, s50) x 10

Compute stfbtotl = sum (f1, f2, f3, f4, f5, f6)

Compute stfbneut = mean (x3, x5, x13, x16, x20, x21, x22, x24, x42, x45, x62, x64, x80, x83,x94, x98) x 10

Compute stfbunds = mean (x9, x25, x31, x34, x35, x40, x52, x53, x59, x65, x68, x76, x82, x84,x92, x97) x 10

Compute stfbdiff = (stfbunds - stfbneut)

See Appendix B for determination of T Scores for the STFB scales.

STFB FACTOR T SCORES

T score 1 _____ T score 2 _____ T score 3 _____ T score 4 _____

T score 5 _____ T score 6 _____

T score Total _____ T score Neutral _____ T score Undesirable _____

T score Neutral – Undesirable Difference _____

STFB PROFILE

Factor Number	Scale Numbers					Factor Score
F1	S1 _____	S2 _____	S3 _____	S4 _____	S5 _____	
	S6 _____	S7 _____	S8 _____	S9 _____	S10 _____	F! _____
F2	S11 _____	S12 _____	S13 _____	S14 _____	S15 _____	
	S16 _____	S17 _____	S18 _____	S19 _____	S20 _____	
	S21 _____					F2 _____
F3	S22 _____	S23 _____	S24 _____	S25 _____	S26 _____	
	S27 _____	S28 _____	S29 _____	S30 _____		F3 _____
F4	S31 _____	S32 _____	S33 _____	S34 _____		F4 _____
F5	S35 _____	S36 _____	S37 _____	S38 _____	S39 _____	
	S40 _____	S41 _____	S42 _____	S43 _____		F5 _____
F6	S44 _____	S45 _____	S46 _____	S47 _____	S48	
	S49 _____	S50 _____				F6 _____

Raw Neutral _____ Raw Undesirable _____ N − U
Difference _____

43

STFB FACTOR T SCORES (FROM APPENDIX B)

T score 1 _____ T score 2 _____ T score 3 _____
T score 4 _____

T score 5 _____ T score 6 _____

T score Total _____ T score Neutral _____ T score
Undesirable _____

T score Neutral – Undesirable Difference _____

APPENDIX B

T-SCORE CONVERSION TABLES FOR THE STFB SCALES

T-Score Conversions for <u>STFB</u> Total (all ages)

RAW SCORE	Male 14-15	Female 14-15	Male 16-17	Female 16-17	Male 18-29	Female 18-29	Male 30-44	Female 30-44
100	112	100	99	111	95	110	110	127
99	111	99	98	110	94	109	109	126
98	110	99	97	109	93	108	108	125
97	109	98	96	108	92	107	107	124
96	108	97	95	108	91	106	106	123
95	107	96	94	107	91	105	106	122
94	105	96	94	106	90	104	105	121
93	104	95	93	105	89	103	104	119
92	103	94	92	104	88	102	103	118
91	102	93	91	103	88	101	102	117
90	101	92	90	102	87	101	101	116
89	100	92	89	101	86	100	100	115
88	99	91	88	100	85	99	99	114
87	98	90	87	99	84	98	98	113
86	97	89	87	98	84	97	97	112
85	96	88	86	97	83	96	96	111
84	95	88	85	96	82	95	95	109
83	94	87	84	95	81	94	95	108
82	93	86	83	95	81	93	94	107
81	92	85	82	94	80	92	93	106
80	91	85	81	93	79	91	92	105
79	90	84	80	92	78	90	91	104

78	89	83	80	91	78	89	90	103
77	88	82	79	90	77	88	89	102
76	87	81	78	89	76	87	88	101
75	86	81	77	88	75	86	87	99
74	85	80	76	87	75	85	86	98
73	84	79	75	86	74	84	85	97
72	83	78	74	85	73	83	84	96
71	82	77	73	84	72	83	84	95
70	81	77	73	83	71	82	83	94
69	80	76	72	82	71	81	82	93
68	79	75	71	81	70	80	81	92
67	78	74	70	81	69	79	80	90
66	77	73	69	80	68	78	79	89
65	76	73	68	79	68	77	78	88
64	75	72	67	78	67	76	77	87
63	74	71	66	77	66	75	76	86
62	73	70	66	76	65	74	75	85
61	72	70	65	75	65	73	74	84
60	71	69	64	74	64	72	73	83
59	70	68	63	73	63	71	72	82
58	69	67	62	72	62	70	72	80
57	68	66	61	71	61	69	71	79
56	67	66	60	70	61	68	70	78
55	66	65	59	69	60	67	69	77
54	65	64	59	68	59	66	68	76
53	64	63	58	68	58	65	67	75
52	63	62	57	67	58	64	66	74
51	62	62	56	66	57	64	65	73
50	61	61	55	65	56	63	64	71
49	60	60	54	64	55	62	63	70
48	59	59	53	63	55	61	62	69
47	58	59	52	62	54	60	61	68
46	57	58	52	61	53	59	61	67
45	56	57	51	60	52	58	60	66
44	55	56	50	59	51	57	59	65
43	54	55	49	58	51	56	58	64
42	52	55	48	57	50	55	57	63
41	51	54	47	56	49	54	56	61
40	50	53	46	55	48	53	55	60
39	49	52	45	54	48	52	54	59

38	48	51	45	54	47	51	53	58
37	47	51	44	53	46	50	52	57
36	46	50	43	52	45	49	51	56
35	45	49	42	51	44	48	50	55
34	44	48	41	50	44	47	50	54
33	43	47	40	49	43	46	49	53
32	42	47	39	48	42	46	48	51
31	41	46	38	47	41	45	47	50
30	40	45	38	46	41	44	46	49
29	39	44	37	45	40	43	45	48
28	38	44	36	44	39	42	44	47
27	37	43	35	43	38	41	43	46
26	36	42	34	42	38	40	42	45
25	35	41	33	41	37	39	41	44
24	34	40	32	41	36	38	40	42
23	33	40	31	40	35	37	39	41
22	32	39	31	39	34	36	39	40
21	31	38	30	38	34	35	38	39
20	30	37	29	37	33	34	37	38
19	29	36	28	36	32	33	36	37
18	28	36	27	35	31	32	35	36
17	27	35	26	34	31	31	34	35
16	26	34	25	33	30	30	33	34
15	25	33	24	32	29	29	32	32
14	24	33	24	31	28	28	31	31
13	23	32	23	30	28	27	30	30
12	22	31	22	29	27	27	29	29
11	21	30	21	28	26	26	28	28
10	20	29	20	27	25	25	27	27
9	19	29	19	27	24	24	27	26
8	18	28	18	26	24	23	26	25
7	17	27	17	25	23	22	25	23
6	16	26	17	24	22	21	24	22
5	15	25	16	23	21	20	23	21
4	14	25	15	22	21	19	22	20
3	13	24	14	21	20	18	21	19
2	12	23	13	20	19	17	20	18
1	11	22	12	19	18	16	19	17

T-Score Conversions for <u>STFB</u> Total (College Students and College Graduates)

RAW SCORE	T Score Using Norms for Male college students	T Score Using Norms for Female college students	T Score Using Norms for Male College students	T Score Using Norms for Female College Students
100	110	121	119	128
99	109	120	118	127
98	108	119	117	126
97	107	118	116	125
96	106	117	115	124
95	105	116	114	123
94	104	115	113	122
93	103	114	112	121
92	102	113	111	119
91	101	112	110	118
90	101	111	109	117
89	100	110	108	116
88	99	108	107	115
87	98	107	106	114
86	97	106	105	113
85	96	105	104	112
84	95	104	103	111
83	94	103	102	110
82	93	102	101	109
81	92	101	100	108
80	91	100	99	106
79	90	99	98	105
78	89	98	97	104
77	88	97	96	103
76	87	96	95	102
75	86	95	94	101

74	85	94	93	100
73	84	93	92	99
72	83	92	91	98
71	82	91	90	97
70	81	90	89	96
69	80	89	88	95
68	79	88	87	94
67	78	87	86	92
66	77	86	85	91
65	76	85	84	90
64	75	84	83	89
63	74	83	82	88
62	73	82	81	87
61	72	81	80	86
60	71	79	79	85
59	70	78	78	84
58	69	77	77	83
57	68	76	76	82
56	67	75	75	81
55	66	74	74	79
54	65	73	73	78
53	64	72	72	77
52	64	71	71	76
51	63	70	70	75
50	62	69	69	74
49	61	68	68	73
48	60	67	67	72
47	59	66	66	71
46	58	65	65	70
45	57	64	64	69
44	56	63	63	68
43	55	62	62	67
42	54	61	61	65
41	53	60	60	64
40	52	59	59	63
39	51	58	58	62
38	50	57	57	61

37	49	56	56	60
36	48	55	55	59
35	47	54	54	58
34	46	53	53	57
33	45	51	52	56
32	44	50	51	55
31	43	49	50	54
30	42	48	49	52
29	41	47	48	51
28	40	46	47	50
27	39	45	46	49
26	38	44	45	48
25	37	43	44	47
24	36	42	43	46
23	35	41	42	45
22	34	40	41	44
21	33	39	40	43
20	32	38	39	42
19	31	37	38	41
18	30	36	37	40
17	29	35	36	38
16	28	34	35	37
15	27	33	34	36
14	26	32	33	35
13	26	31	32	34
12	25	30	31	33
11	24	29	30	32
10	23	28	29	31
9	22	27	28	30
8	21	26	27	29
7	20	25	26	28
6	19	24	25	27
5	18	22	24	25
4	17	21	23	24
3	16	20	22	23
2	15	19	21	22
1	14	18	20	21

T-Score Conversions
(Adolescent Males Ages 14 and 15)

RAW SCORE	F1	F2	F3	F4	F5	F6	$\underline{N}$eut.	$\underline{U}$ndes.	Diff. (N-U)
22		98							
21		94							
20	90	90							
19	87	86							
18	83	82	101		98				
17	80	78	96		93				
16	77	74	91		89		92	93	102
15	74	70	87		85		87	89	98
14	70	66	82		81	81	83	85	95
13	67	62	78		76	77	78	81	91
12	64	58	73		72	73	74	77	87
11	61	54	69		68	69	70	73	84
10	58	50	64		64	65	65	69	80
9	54	46	60		59	61	61	65	77
8	51	42	55	108	55	57	56	62	73
7	48	38	51	98	51	53	52	58	69
6	45	34	46	89	47	49	47	54	66
5	42	30	41	79	42	44	43	50	62
4	38	26	37	70	38	40	38	46	59
3	35	22	32	60	34	36	34	42	55
2	32	18	28	51	30	32	30	38	52
1	29	14	23	41	25	28	25	34	48

T-Score Conversions
(Adolescent Females Ages 14 and 15)

RAW SCORE	F1	F2	F3	F4	F5	F6	N̲eut.	U̲ndes.	Diff. (N-U)
22		82							
21		80							
20	86	77							
19	84	75							
18	81	72	90		93				
17	78	70	87		89				
16	75	67	83		85		89	85	99
15	72	65	80		82		85	82	96
14	69	62	77		78	91	81	79	92
13	66	60	73		74	86	77	76	89
12	63	57	70		71	81	73	73	86
11	61	54	67		67	77	69	70	82
10	58	52	63		63	72	65	67	79
9	55	49	60		59	67	62	64	76
8	52	47	57	101	56	62	58	60	72
7	49	44	53	93	52	57	54	57	69
6	46	42	50	85	48	52	50	54	65
5	43	39	47	77	45	47	46	51	62
4	40	37	43	69	41	43	42	48	59
3	38	34	40	60	37	38	38	45	55
2	35	32	37	52	34	33	34	42	52
1	32	29	33	44	30	28	30	39	49

T-Score Conversions
(Adolescent Males Ages 16 and 17)

RAW SCORE	F1	F2	F3	F4	F5	F6	N̲ eut.	U̲ ndes.	Diff. (N-U)
22		81							
21		79							
20	81	76							
19	78	73							
18	76	70	91		89				
17	73	68	87		85				
16	70	65	84		81		85	90	102
15	67	62	80		77		81	86	98
14	64	60	76		73	78	77	82	95
13	61	57	72		69	74	72	79	91
12	58	54	68		65	70	68	75	87
11	56	52	64		61	66	64	71	83
10	53	50	60		57	62	60	67	80
9	50	46	56		53	58	55	63	76
8	47	44	53	93	49	54	51	59	72
7	44	41	49	86	45	50	47	55	68
6	41	38	45	78	41	46	43	51	65
5	38	36	41	71	37	42	38	48	61
4	36	33	37	63	33	39	34	44	57
3	33	30	33	56	29	35	30	40	53
2	30	27	29	48	25	31	26	36	50
1	27	25	25	41	21	27	21	32	56

T-Score Conversions
(Adolescent Females Ages 16 and 17)

RAW SCORE	F1	F2	F3	F4	F5	F6	N eut.	U ndes.	Diff. (N-U)
22		96							
21		93							
20	95	89							
19	92	86							
18	89	82	90		99				
17	86	79	86		95				
16	82	75	83		91		97	96	100
15	79	72	80		87		93	92	97
14	76	69	76		82	87	88	88	93
13	73	65	73		78	83	83	84	90
12	69	62	70		74	78	79	80	86
11	66	58	67		70	74	74	77	83
10	63	55	63		65	69	70	73	79
9	60	51	60		61	64	65	69	76
8	56	48	57	110	57	60	60	65	72
7	53	45	53	101	53	55	56	61	69
6	50	41	50	92	49	51	51	57	65
5	47	38	47	83	44	46	47	54	62
4	43	34	43	74	40	42	42	50	58
3	40	31	40	65	36	37	37	46	54
2	37	27	37	56	32	32	33	42	51
1	34	24	33	47	28	28	28	38	47

T-Score Conversions
(Adult Males Ages 18 to 29)

RAW SCORE	F1	F2	F3	F4	F5	F6	N eut.	U ndes.	Diff. (N-U)
22		77							
21		75							
20	91	73							
19	88	70							
18	84	68	83		96				
17	81	65	80		92				
16	77	63	77		87		92	82	93
15	74	61	74		83		87	79	90
14	71	58	71		79	78	82	76	87
13	67	56	68		75	74	78	73	84
12	64	53	65		70	70	73	70	81
11	60	51	62		66	66	68	67	78
10	57	49	59		62	62	63	64	75
9	54	46	56		57	58	58	61	72
8	50	44	53	85	53	54	54	58	69
7	47	41	50	79	49	50	49	55	66
6	43	39	47	73	45	46	44	52	63
5	40	37	44	67	40	42	39	49	60
4	37	34	41	60	36	38	34	46	57
3	33	32	38	54	32	34	30	43	54
2	30	29	35	48	28	30	25	40	51
1	26	27	32	42	23	26	20	36	48

T-Score Conversions
(Adult Females Ages 18 to 29)

RAW SCORE	F1	F2	F3	F4	F5	F6	N eut.	U ndes.	Diff. (N-U)
22		83							
21		81							
20	86	78							
19	83	75							
18	81	73	114		103				
17	78	70	108		99				
16	75	67	103		94		97	91	94
15	73	64	98		90		92	87	91
14	70	62	92		85	86	87	84	88
13	67	59	87		80	81	82	80	85
12	64	56	82		76	77	77	77	82
11	62	54	76		71	72	72	73	78
10	59	51	71		67	67	67	69	75
9	56	48	66		62	63	61	66	72
8	53	45	60	94	58	58	56	62	69
7	51	43	55	87	53	53	51	58	66
6	48	40	50	80	48	48	46	55	63
5	45	37	44	73	44	44	41	51	59
4	43	35	39	67	39	39	36	47	56
3	40	32	34	60	35	34	31	44	53
2	37	29	28	53	30	30	26	40	50
1	34	27	23	46	26	25	21	36	47

T-Score Conversions
(Adult Males Ages 30 to 44)

RAW SCORE	F1	F2	F3	F4	F5	F6	N̲ eut.	U̲ ndes.	Diff. (N-U)
22		96							
21		92							
20	90	88							
19	87	85							
18	84	81	90		102				
17	82	78	87		98				
16	79	74	84		93		94	98	95
15	76	71	80		89		89	94	91
14	73	67	77		85	91	84	90	88
13	70	64	74		81	87	79	86	84
12	67	60	70		76	82	75	82	81
11	64	57	67		72	77	70	78	77
10	62	53	64		68	72	65	74	74
9	59	50	60		63	68	60	70	70
8	56	46	57	96	59	63	55	66	67
7	53	43	54	88	55	58	51	62	64
6	50	39	50	80	50	53	46	59	60
5	47	35	47	72	46	48	41	55	57
4	44	32	44	64	42	44	36	51	53
3	42	28	40	56	37	39	31	47	50
2	39	25	37	48	33	34	27	43	46
1	36	21	34	40	29	29	22	39	43

T-Score Conversions
(Adult Females Ages 29 to 44)

RAW SCORE	F1	F2	F3	F4	F5	F6	N̲ eut.	U̲ ndes.	Diff. (N-U)
22		112							
21		108							
20	101	103							
19	97	99							
18	94	94	99		101				
17	90	90	95		97				
16	87	85	91		93		87	117	91
15	83	81	87		89		83	112	88
14	80	76	83		85	99	79	107	85
13	77	72	80		81	93	75	101	81
12	73	67	76		77	87	72	96	78
11	70	63	72		73	81	68	91	75
10	66	58	68		69	76	64	85	72
9	63	54	64		65	70	60	80	69
8	60	49	60	99	61	64	56	75	66
7	56	45	57	91	57	59	53	69	63
6	53	40	53	84	53	53	49	64	60
5	49	36	49	77	48	47	45	58	57
4	46	31	45	70	44	41	41	53	53
3	43	27	41	63	40	36	37	48	50
2	39	22	37	55	36	30	34	42	47
1	36	18	33	48	32	24	30	37	44

T-Score Conversions
(Male College Students)

RAW SCORE	F1	F2	F3	F4	F5	F6	N eut.	U ndes.	Diff. (N-U)
22		88							
21		85							
20	86	82							
19	83	79							
18	80	76	91		101				
17	77	73	88		97				
16	74	70	84		93		86	91	90
15	71	67	80		88		82	88	87
14	69	63	77		84	95	79	84	84
13	66	60	73		79	89	75	80	81
12	63	57	69		75	84	71	77	78
11	60	54	66		71	78	67	73	75
10	57	51	62		66	73	63	70	72
9	54	48	59		62	67	59	66	70
8	51	45	55	90	57	61	55	62	67
7	48	41	51	84	53	56	51	59	64
6	45	38	48	77	49	50	47	55	61
5	42	35	44	71	44	45	43	52	58
4	39	32	40	64	40	39	39	48	55
3	36	29	37	58	35	34	36	45	52
2	33	26	33	51	31	28	32	41	49
1	31	23	30	45	27	23	28	37	47

T-Score Conversions
(Female College Students)

RAW SCORE	F1	F2	F3	F4	F5	F6	N eut.	U ndes.	Diff. (N-U)
22		98							
21		95							
20	101	91							
19	97	88							
18	94	84	100		111				
17	90	81	96		106				
16	87	77	92		101		96	102	97
15	84	73	88		96		92	98	93
14	80	70	84		91	93	88	94	90
13	77	66	80		86	88	83	90	86
12	73	63	76		81	83	79	86	83
11	70	59	72		76	78	74	82	79
10	67	56	68		71	73	70	78	76
9	63	52	64		66	68	65	74	73
8	60	48	60	103	61	63	61	70	69
7	56	45	56	95	56	58	56	66	66
6	53	41	52	87	51	53	52	62	62
5	50	38	48	79	46	48	48	58	59
4	46	34	44	71	41	43	43	54	55
3	43	31	40	63	36	38	39	50	52
2	39	27	36	55	31	33	34	46	48
1	36	23	32	47	27	29	30	42	45

T-Score Conversions
(Male College Graduates)

RAW SCORE	F1	F2	F3	F4	F5	F6	N eut.	U ndes.	Diff. (N-U)
22		96							
21		93							
20	100	90							
19	97	86							
18	93	83	105		103				
17	89	80	101		99				
16	86	76	96		94		99	102	98
15	82	73	92		90		94	98	95
14	78	70	88		86	88	89	94	91
13	74	66	84		82	84	84	90	87
12	71	63	80		78	80	80	86	84
11	67	60	75		74	75	75	82	80
10	63	57	71		70	71	70	78	76
9	60	53	67		66	67	65	74	73
8	56	50	63	107	62	62	61	70	69
7	52	47	59	98	58	58	56	66	65
6	49	43	54	89	54	54	51	62	62
5	45	40	50	81	50	49	46	58	58
4	41	37	46	72	46	45	42	54	54
3	38	33	42	64	42	41	37	50	51
2	34	30	38	55	38	36	32	46	47
1	30	27	33	46	34	32	27	42	44

T-Score Conversions
(Female College Graduates)

RAW SCORE	F1	F2	F3	F4	F5	F6	N eut.	U ndes.	Diff. (N-U)
22		100							
21		97							
20	118	93							
19	113	90							
18	109	86	115		106				
17	104	83	110		102				
16	100	80	105		97		112	115	104
15	96	76	100		93		105	110	100
14	91	73	95		89	95	99	105	96
13	87	70	90		85	90	93	101	91
12	82	66	86		80	85	87	96	86
11	78	63	81		76	80	81	91	82
10	73	59	76		72	75	75	87	78
9	69	56	71		68	70	69	82	74
8	65	53	66	116	64	65	63	77	69
7	60	49	61	107	59	60	57	72	65
6	56	46	56	97	55	55	51	68	61
5	51	42	51	87	51	50	45	63	56
4	47	39	46	77	47	45	39	58	52
3	43	36	42	67	42	40	33	53	48
2	38	32	37	57	38	35	27	49	43
1	34	29	32	47	34	30	21	44	39

APPENDIX C

Description of Some of the Treatment Components

In this appendix, we would like to tell you a bit about some of the treatment methods employed in this study, since the average clinician may not be familiar with them. These descriptions are intended to be illustrative only, and anyone who cares to duplicate these programs in other settings should refer to the original works from which these procedures were drawn.

Cognitive Restructuring/Reframing: Guilt feelings are experiences in which everybody shares. Guilt is learned early in life as a result of reproval and criticism, and it serves as a means to remind the child to inhibit some actions in order to avoid pain from the future consequences of his actions. The reproval is offered as an act of love, seeking to protect the child from injury and embarrassment, but it is commonly misunderstood as evidence of absence of love. Guilt, and the incorporation of self-depreciation and fearful avoidance of other's judgements about "mistakes," may be taken to heart. Consequently, most of us know more about our "bad" than our "good" selves. Each of us has been "bad" for much less than one percent of his or her life. Others' and our own guilt-provoking judgements are simply wrong. Guilt is the judgement now that a past event should have been done differently. But it could not have been done differently. Everybody always does the very best he or she can at every moment, given the circumstances and the person's condition, including both the parents and oneself. Therefore, since nothing could have been done differently, we are all perfect. Indeed, perhaps the only real sin is guilt itself. The loving intention behind a guilt-trip, and the fact that the judgement made is always wrong, suggests that guilt-trips could be enjoyed.

Similarly, everybody feels or thinks he has failed at times. Mostly, failure is a judgement made by others which we believe to the extent we value the others or their opinions. We expect to be punished or put-down by others for our failures, and we sometimes take on the role of judging ourselves either to avoid failures or to anticipate punishment (punishing ourselves). But there really is no such thing as failure; only feedback. In addition to the fact that we all always do the very best we can, we are all magnificent learning machines, and everybody is always growing and improving his skills and actions every moment of every day. The trouble has been that we have been raised in a society which over-values competition – in the family, at school, in sports, in activities, with friends, and even in court. For example, we who are in jail are all failures in competing with the prosecution, i.e., defending ourselves before the Law. But society hasn't "got it": competition is one of the main sources of war and of crime. Identify (on paper) several repeating situations in which you most either feel like a "failure" or fear failing. Take each in turn and (a) reverse your view of failure in it into success – enjoy the fun of trying to fail or make the mistake, and (b) reverse the contingencies involving failure – enjoy trying as an objective to achieve the very thing you fear may happen (Use examples such as Ellis' "objective" of being turned down as often as possible in requests for dates.) Pair off in dyads to play the game of enjoying failing.

Everybody feels a certain amount of distress every day, and a great deal of distress from time to time. Suppose you had no means at all by which you could reduce your distress. You would live with it and tolerate it, right? In fact, one of the things that sets us up to risk becoming addicts is that we think we can't stand our distresses, and that we have to get rid of them NOW. (Examples, such as being scared while driving, and the consequences of stopping and leaving the car versus keeping on driving.) We can all tolerate distress just fine and, if we do, it passes – almost never lasts longer than 90 minutes. In fact, let's have some fun enjoying distress.

Wouldn't it be nice to enjoy being free ... to be warm, friendly, concerned and close with everybody. The trouble is you can't trust any person ... to be consistently caring the whole time. (Use the logic of Pascal's Wager to demonstrate it is always a mistake of thinking not to trust other people with your feelings.) (Use "the love test tube" model (Quirk, 1991) to explain how it gets to be hard to trust, and easy to create "distance" from others emotionally.) So we all make mistakes of thinking which create havoc and trouble in our lives. It might be well to examine some of our mistakes of thinking, and even how we could find ways out of our problems.

Thought is the single main source of personal distress and thus interpersonal and other trouble. Thought is always a waste of time. In fact, when we are wasting time, the way we keep ourselves from boredom is commonly by thinking. Thought, however, never has to do with reality, if only in that by the time we think about the present, the present is already past. What happens to many of us, who have been taught that we ought to think and that our thoughts should be organized, is that we confuse ourselves trying to organize our thoughts. Another use we often make of thinking is to manufacture faults in ourselves and others, and we justify our fault-finding on the grounds that we have been trained that it is desirable to maintain a critical attitude of mind – it is not. By finding fault we manage to find ways to disrespect others, and thus to justify our cold and distant attitudes toward others by which we avoid "getting close" to others. Finally, we often use thought to find justifications, rationalizations, excuses and intellectualizations about ourselves and what we do. Of course, since there are as many different logics as there are people, nobody except ourselves is convinced by our impeccable arguments and incisive logic. Just because thought is a waste of time, however, does not mean that cautiousness and precision should not be used in the things we say and do. We can enjoy being cautious and precise. But we don't need any "self-control," or to concern ourselves about the ways we think others want us to "conform." Our brains are already programmed beautifully, so that we will do what we are going to do whether or not we have thought it through first, and no matter how much self-control we exercise. Of course, self-control too can be fun. Use it for that purpose. Most of what we believe and say is achieved through the exercise of what we are pleased to call "common sense." All that "common sense" really tends to mean is that we jumped to a conclusion on the strength of impression, emotional attitude and imagined consensus of opinion – that is, attitudes we think are in fashion or are popular. Common sense commonly misleads us all. It is probably true that, if a million people believe something, it is bound to be wrong. We are all in jail. This means that our freedoms and choices have been denied us, and we are restricted from doing anything interesting or useful, right? Wrong! There is just as much freedom in jail as in any other life setting. Freedom is only the freedom to choose or decide. But we can't decide freely to go home or any number of other things. Of course we can. The only thing that restricts us is our own unwillingness to accept the consequences of making certain choices. We restrict ourselves because we aren't willing to pay the costs of making certain decisions. But that's always true for everybody, at every moment of his life. Moreover, in jail we actually have MORE freedom than on the street. We are free from the requirements of supporting ourselves, those complexities which we don't handle well of deciding how to use our leisure time, the demands of life's distractions by which we prevent ourselves from pursuing our own best interests and things which might later contribute to the quality of our lives and, for some of us, from the constraints imposed by our relationships with others – that is, we are free to make new lives for ourselves with new choices about those we will relate to in various ways. So, maybe it's time, while you have the opportunity freely to feel confined, to enjoy your restraints.

Actually, all confinement and restraint comes from within ourselves. Even when prevented movement of our bodies, we are free to exercise our minds – where all of anybody's reality exists. Inhibition comes mainly from thought, but also from habits of self-control and of avoidance. Since action and thought compete with one another, the confinement that comes through thought impedes the use of the body's energy – the body is just an energy-producing machine. The felt restraint from this source creates an increased pressure for bodily energy to be used, which can eventually lead to a sense of rage. To combat rage, use up the body's energies in actions (restlessness, pacing, exercise or any vital activity). Self-control is necessary, right? It is not. We are well-programmed to act as we will act, and all the extra burden of self-control does is increase the ANS-stress arousal which increases anger. Trust your well-programmed brain and enjoy doing crazy things. Avoidance habits are learned to keep us from doing things we fear, but the fear and the avoidance result in situations and reactions of ours which result in robbing ourselves of joy and justifying for ourselves hostile attitudes and feelings toward others. We live in an engineered safe society. There is nothing to fear, except the effects of fear itself.

"Personal Development" Goals Development (Quirk, 1993): To discover your perfection, take on the job of noticing and rewarding your "goodness" so that you become your "Ideal Self." List all the qualities you would like as your ideal self. Under each quality, list a half-dozen observable behaviours which define that quality. Each morning read over the behaviours to remind yourself of them. During the day reward yourself ("pat on the back"), and even record, every time you notice yourself, even for an instant, doing any (even) approximation to any act on your lists. You will soon discover how good you are, and become your ideal self.

Values Development (James and Woodsmall, 1987): List all your values – everybody has lots – and extend them to include as many "replicative" (positive only) values as you can. If unfamiliar with considering your values, you might consider those listed in the multiple-choice values checklist (Quirk, 1992) – made available to the participants. Values are the most general guides for living, the best means for self-definition, the motivators which determine how we use our time, the means by which we evaluate how we have done (thus, values underlie guilt feelings), and the most abstract or general issues affecting everything in our lives. It is well worthwhile discovering and developing your own values.

The "Visual Squash" (James and Woodsmall, 1987): Consider "guilt" and its opposite (e.g., "innocence"). What picture pops to mind when you think of guilt? What picture pops to mind when you think of its opposite? Close your eyes and hold out your hands, palms up. Choose one hand on which to place the picture of "guilt." Place the picture of its opposite on the other hand. They are both "parts of you" (images through which you process personal experiences) and they are placed on your hands to externalize them so you can talk to parts of you and know which parts you are talking to. Ask the "guilt" part what its highest intention for you is ... and why does it want that for you? ... Ask the opposite part what its highest intention for you is ..., and why does it want that for you? ... (Proceed according to the method outlined by James).

The "Swish" (Bandler, 1985; Andreas and Andreas, 1987): Picture a common situation in which someone tries to "lay a guilt-trip on you." Set that picture aside for the moment. Picture yourself feeling just the way you would want to feel – confident, relaxed, etc. Now, with the camera of your eye, zoom the picture off into the distance, way off until it is just a dot on the horizon. Bring the "guilt-trip" picture back in front of you, then zoom it out to the horizon at the same time as you zoom the other picture (the one of yourself looking just the way you would wish to feel) back in again. Look at it closely. Let that scene fade away, and then do it all over again, but faster. Picture a common situation in which someone tries to "lay a guilt-trip on you." Set that picture aside for the moment. Picture yourself feeling just the way you would want to feel – confident, relaxed, etc. Now, with the camera of your eye, zoom the picture off into the distance, way off until it is just a dot on the horizon. Bring the "guilt-trip" picture back in front of you, then zoom it out to the horizon at the same time as you zoom the other picture (the one of yourself looking just the way you would wish to feel) back in again. Look at it closely. Let that scene fade away, and then do it all over again. Repeat this process, switching the pictures very, very quickly – swish – half a dozen times, or until even the very thought of guilt-trips makes you think of feeling confident and relaxed.

"Time Line" (Andreas and Andreas, 1987; James and Woodsmall, 1987): Everything exists in your mind, in images of the past, present and future. Imagine your past to be a long series of pictures stored in order so you can tell which came ahead of which. Imagine your future as a series of pictures of possible future events – future memories, as it were. Imagine a line running forward through the past pictures, through the present, and on through the future pictures. Leave that line of pictures where it is, and drift up, way up, above that line. Look down and see the line below. Drift down to just above the line, and float back until you're over a time when you first felt guilty about anything (a time ...). Float farther back in time, say another fifteen or twenty minutes or so, and turn so that you are facing the present with that memory below you and in front of you. Where are those feelings of guilt now? (If you still feel guilty ...). Step forward, with your adult understandings and resources, into that first experience, and notice how you feel. When you're ready, move on through similar events toward the present only as fast as you can experience that and each similar situation with peace and relaxation.

Media-Proofing: In adulthood, one of our most usual ways of comparing our lives with those of others is through the eye of the media, especially T.V. But the world as shown to us in the media is entirely make-believe. (Data on the distortions of reality found in the media, e.g., murder rates and characteristics, sex and race roles, etc., etc.) Our expectations are shaped by the lifestyles of people as they seem to be in the media. Life is just not like that. For example, each of you has heard and told stories about all the violent acts you and your fellow inmates have been involved with. For your own stories, you know they are rarely ever true; and the same is true of others' stories. We all believe there is much more violence out there than we have ever experienced. So we make up for the imagined deficiencies in our lives. (Data on the effects of exposure to the media on people's lives and behaviours.)

"Achievement" Goals (Quirk, 1993): The essences of a method to develop (linear) achievement goals, objectives and action plans for one's own life are shown, with special emphasis on checking off action plans as completed. Examples of today's accomplishments are given.

Cumulative Frequency Graphs: The use of cumulative frequencies to display all sorts of recorded actions and experiences is illustrated, and recording sheets and graphs are provided with suggestions about events to tally and how to use the tallies and the graphs.

Meditation: The largest source of distress for everybody is thinking – our thoughts are what upset us. But how can you stop thinking? Don't think about a purple hippopotamus. To NOT think of it, you must think of it. In fact, nobody can do a not-do. But it is possible to reduce the pressure of thinking, and thus disturbance from thoughts, greatly. You can do it by thinking ... about something that has no meaning to you. But everything you can think of means something, right? One thing that means nothing might be a word from a language you don't know. Sanskrit in a dead language that nobody knows, so any word from it, listened to, might distract you from other thoughts. Some methods for meditation are explained and tried briefly, with a focus on Transcendental Meditation (T.M.).

Stress Management Training: Explanation of how the ANS works, with particular emphasis on breathing IN as a sympathetic response and breathing OUT as a parasympathetic response. Long out-breaths (NOT deep breaths) are explained and practised for their effects in creating calmness.

Relaxation Training (Jacobson, 1938): Specific muscle-group progressive muscle relaxation training is selected to permit controlled group relaxation, and explanation and practice in it is provided.

Systematic Desensitization (Wolpe, 1958): All participants are induced to relax, and relaxation-mediated desensitization (sometimes enhanced by eye-movement desensitization) is employed, using "standard hierarchies" of anxiety and distress stimuli common among offenders, and asking for hand-raising signals if anyone's SUD (Subjective Units of Discomfort) level exceeds 30 on a 100 point scale. Any presentation is terminated when anyone in the group either raises his hand or exhibits "voluntary" restlessness.

"Rapid Phobia Treatment" (Bandler and Grinder, 1979; Bandler, 1985; Andreas and Andreas, 1989): Select a situation in which you might feel upset. Make a video movie of it, starting from when you feel safe, and ending with you in a safe place. Make a theatre, and seat yourself in it looking at the screen. Drift up and out of yourself, leaving yourself in the theatre, and drifting up into the projection booth. Look down from the projection booth at the you in the theatre watching the screen to watch how the you in the theatre reacts. Ask the projectionist to run the film you made on the screen fairly quickly through in black-and-white. How did the you in the theatre seem to feel? (If uncomfortable, drift up and out of yourself in the projection booth and ...) Ask the projectionist to rewind the film fast, in colour so that everything happens in reverse. How did the you in the theatre seem to feel? Repeat the process several times. Drift back down to sit beside the you in the theatre and watch that you more closely. Repeat the process. Drift back into yourself in the theatre. Repeat the process. Drift up into the action on the screen, playing your role in it. Repeat the process.

Rational-Emotive Therapy (Ellis and Harper, 1961, 1975): Having handed out a Beliefs Inventory and a Resiliency Inventory to be completed (during the inter-hour break), the inventories are now self-scored, and common errors of thinking identified are examined. The suggestion is made that both inventories be repeated often, each time thoughtfully considering whether each item answered in the direction of "error" or "non-resiliency" could be thought of differently, and only changing the answer given if it is honestly believed to be in the other direction at that time. To the extent that you can "change your mind" on any item, to that extent you either reduce the extent to which you upset yourself with "error" ideas, or increase the freedom and ease with which you adapt to life's changing circumstances. Either improves quality of living.

Problem Solving: How many of you are "stuck" in acting or thinking in a particular way, or cannot solve a problem in your lives? How come? The answer is simply that we keep using the same strategies in life over and over again, or that we have not yet found the right strategies to achieve what we want to do. The role of language and words in creating and perpetuating problems is outlined. The role of sentence syntax, especially negative format instructions, is outlined and solutions suggested. The consequent reliance on avoidant strategies is outlined and alternatives discussed. The role of externalizing responsibilities and control is illustrated and reframed.

Enhancing Functioning: In that a central theme in Factor 4 has to do with concrete and simplistic thought, apparently associated with motivated insensitivity, some training is offered in intelligence functioning to foster improved success in problem-solving and human interactions. A few exercises and strategies are introduced to enhance concept-formation and thus abstract thinking, perceptual acuity and discrimination, and thus accuracy of responses, and mnemonics to aid in retention and retrieval of information.

Assertiveness Training (Lange and Jakubowski, 1976; Jakubowski and Lange, 1978): In addition to the usual elements of assertive training programs (the nature of assertiveness, "I" statements, 3-part statements, etc.), a particular emphasis is placed on (1) the use of bodily energy (in exercise, vocal impact on the environment, definiteness of statement, clarity of enunciation, etc.), and (2) the syntax of linguistics in sending communications (brevity of sentences to exclude explanatory clauses, positive and permissive statements to counter negative format statements and criticality, decisiveness in instant response to counter rumination and foster trusting of the good programming of one's brain, rapidity of repartee to enhance activity and energy use, etc.) "Mottos" are offered as aids to application, such as "Never explain. Your friends don't need it, and your enemies won't believe it anyway."

Assertive Training II: Personal rights, common to many assertive training programs, are presented and explained, along with extended focus on freedom in using the body's energies, particularly the energies of emotions and loving. Participants list recurring situations, in which discomfort, joylessness or strong negative emotions are felt.

72

Under each, 16± alternative possible responses in the situation are listed, ordered in a hierarchy from most aggressive to most under-assertive, with most in the middle. Each list of responses is committed to memory. When one of the situations recurs, stop, run quickly through the associated list of responses, choose the one you would be comfortable with, step one step down from it and deliver that response.

Empathy Training: Methods from Assertive Training are used to enhance "empathy" in responses (sending messages), and extended by training in effective listening and in non-verbal reception and expression. Participants try out listening dyads.

Divergent Thinking: In order to reduce the fixity of ideas commonly encountered in introversive-obsessional-conforming people (part of what Factor 5 seems to represent), encouragement is offered to employ divergent thinking actively, both to provide alternative points of view and to view events with humour and objectivity – Factor 5 people act as though they were "objective" to create "distance" from emotions and from others, but in fact view events in highly subjective ways. Various tools for divergent thinking were offered, including fragments from a Dictionary for Divergent Thinkers (Quirk, 1989).

How to Achieve Joy: (1) Respect everyone. If you choose to respect everyone, you will discover the good in them (always vastly exceeds anything else). But the gifts which flow from giving respect are NOT given to the other person, they are given to yourself by yourself – you find yourself living in a world full of goodness which, contrary to expectations, makes you feel good. (2) Trust everyone. If you choose to trust everyone, contrary to expectations, you will feel safe in life and in human relationships, and the gift of trust is NOT given to others, it is given to you by yourself in feeling safe. (3) It is then possible to love everyone. If you choose to love everyone, your body's energies become invested in everyone and everything around you. The gift of loving is NOT given to the other, it is given to you by yourself, as you find joy for yourself.

Achieving Freedom: Jump up and fly in the air around the room. Accept fair returns for what you have given others – whoops, we all get many times more than we give. Put a sign on your weekly canteen supplies: "Steal all of this." Wear a sign on your back: "Kick me." Do you think that's funny? You do? Good! You have begun to achieve freedom. Whenever you have to do something, play it as a game. Could you do that? You could? Good! You're well on your way. Do you think it's right that people should treat each other as equals? Could you be the first person to act that way? Could you keep it up? You could? Good! You're almost there. Could you start practising the three steps to joy? Could you find three different things you like every time you are moving from one place to another, as a start? You could? Good! When you've done those things for a few short weeks you will have arrived; you will know what freedom is.

Appendix D

In contrast to most correctional research, this study was not a separate entity in itself, since investigations are continuing. New sets of data are being assembled and analysed, and new observations about the structure of criminality are continuing to emerge.

Subsequent to completion of the treatment phase of this study, the STFB scores of a new sample of 1951 inmate-subjects became available for analysis. The scree plot for this sample shows that there are at least three robust factors within this data, and possibly as many as five or six, as was true of the sample on which the original six factors were derived.

However, the fifty 2-item scales absolutely refused to load on the same factors as they had in the original sample! Consequently, in an effort to understand the meaning of the factor structure in this new data set, three-, four-, five- and six-factor solutions were generated, and the scales loading on each of the factors were recorded. Loadings for the fifty STFB item sets on each of the factors are shown in the following tables with a ✓

In addition, given that there are fifty 2-items scales (or sets of items), it was decided to attempt to construct five quasi-factor scales comprised of ten sets of items each. This was done through what might be called successive approximations, by combining into mini-factor scales those sets of items with the highest and most unambiguous loadings on each of five factors; these mini-factor scales were then re-factoring along with the remaining scales (or item-sets); those scales most highly associated with each mini-factor were then added to them and these revised mini-factors were re-factored along with the as-yet- unassigned scales; and the process was repeated until all of the 50 scales were included in one or other of the five quasi-factor scales. Scale loadings on each of these quasi-factor scales are indicated in the following table with an X.

FACTOR LOADINGS OF THE FIFTY 2-ITEM SETS OF STFB ITEMS

Item Set	Factor Solution	Factor 1	Factor 2	Factor 3	Factor 4	Factor 5	Factor 6
1 - reversed - - reversed - - reversed - - reversed -	6-factor 5-factor 4-factor 3-factor		✓ ✓			 ✓ ✓X	
2	6-factor 5-factor 4-factor 3-factor	✓ ✓X ✓ ✓					
3	6-factor 5-factor 4-factor 3-factor	 ✓			✓ ✓X ✓		
4	6-factor 5-factor 4-factor 3-factor			✓ ✓X ✓ ✓			
5	6-factor 5-factor 4-factor 3-factor	✓ ✓X ✓ ✓					
6	6-factor 5-factor 4-factor 3-factor	✓ ✓X ✓ ✓					
7	6-factor 5-factor 4-factor 3-factor	✓ ✓ ✓ ✓		 X			

8	6-factor	✓					
	5-factor	✓X					
	4-factor	✓					
	3-factor	✓					
9	6-factor			✓			
	5-factor		✓	✓		X	
	4-factor			✓			
	3-factor						
10	6-factor						
	5-factor			✓	✓	✓X	✓
	4-factor						
	3-factor						
11	6-factor		✓X				
	5-factor		✓			✓	
	4-factor		✓				
	3-factor		✓				
12	6-factor		✓				
	5-factor		✓X				
	4-factor		✓				
	3-factor		✓				
13	6-factor		✓				
	5-factor		✓X				
	4-factor		✓				
	3-factor		✓				
14	6-factor			✓			
	5-factor			✓X			
	4-factor			✓			
	3-factor			✓			
15	6-factor			✓			
	5-factor			✓	X		✓
	4-factor			✓			
	3-factor						
16	6-factor		✓				
	5-factor		✓		X		
	4-factor		✓				
	3-factor		✓				
17	6-factor			✓			
	5-factor		✓	✓	X		
	4-factor			✓			
	3-factor						

#								
18	6-factor				✓			
	5-factor	✓			✓X			
	4-factor				✓			
	3-factor							
19	6-factor				✓			
	5-factor	✓			✓X			
	4-factor				✓			
	3-factor							
20	6-factor							
	5-factor	✓			X	✓		
	4-factor	✓			✓			
	3-factor							
21	6-factor	✓						
	5-factor	✓		X				
	4-factor	✓						
	3-factor	✓						
22	6-factor	✓						
	5-factor	✓X						
	4-factor	✓						
	3-factor	✓						
23	6-factor		✓					
	5-factor		✓X					
	4-factor		✓					
	3-factor		✓					
24 - reversed -	6-factor		X					
- reversed -	5-factor		✓		✓			
- reversed -	4-factor		✓		✓			
- reversed -	3-factor		✓					
25	6-factor		✓					
	5-factor		✓X					
	4-factor		✓					
	3-factor		✓					
26	6-factor			✓				
	5-factor			✓	X			
	4-factor			✓				
	3-factor			✓				
27	6-factor	✓						
	5-factor	✓	✓		X			
	4-factor	✓						
	3-factor							

28	6-factor			✓			
	5-factor			✓	X		
	4-factor			✓			
	3-factor			✓			
29	6-factor	✓					
	5-factor	✓X					
	4-factor	✓					
	3-factor	✓					
30	6-factor	✓					
	5-factor	✓X					
	4-factor	✓					
	3-factor	✓					
31	6-factor			✓			
	5-factor			✓		X	✓
	4-factor			✓			
	3-factor						
32	6-factor			✓			
	5-factor			✓X			
	4-factor			✓			
	3-factor			✓			
33	6-factor	✓					
	5-factor	✓				X	✓
	4-factor	✓					
	3-factor						
34 - reversed - - reversed - - reversed - - reversed -	6-factor		✓X				
	5-factor		✓			✓	
	4-factor		✓				
	3-factor						
35	6-factor						
	5-factor		✓	✓		X	
	4-factor		✓	✓			
	3-factor						
36	6-factor		✓				
	5-factor		✓X	✓			
	4-factor		✓				
	3-factor						
37	6-factor		✓				
	5-factor		✓X				
	4-factor		✓				
	3-factor		✓				

#	factor						
38	6-factor		✓				
	5-factor		✓X				
	4-factor		✓				
	3-factor		✓				
39 - reversed - - reversed - - reversed - - reversed -	6-factor		✓		✓	X	
	5-factor		✓		✓		
	4-factor						
	3-factor						
40	6-factor			✓			
	5-factor			✓X			
	4-factor			✓			
	3-factor			✓			
41	6-factor			✓			
	5-factor			✓	X		✓
	4-factor			✓			
	3-factor						
42	6-factor	✓					
	5-factor	✓X					
	4-factor	✓					
	3-factor	✓					
43	6-factor	✓					
	5-factor	✓X					
	4-factor	✓					
	3-factor	✓					
44	6-factor				✓		
	5-factor			✓	✓	X	
	4-factor				✓		
	3-factor						
45	6-factor	✓					
	5-factor	✓X					
	4-factor	✓					
	3-factor	✓					
46	6-factor						
	5-factor	✓	✓			✓	
	4-factor					✓X	
	3-factor						
47	6-factor	✓					
	5-factor	✓	✓	X			
	4-factor	✓					
	3-factor						

48	6-factor	✓		X			
	5-factor	✓					
	4-factor	✓					
	3-factor	✓					
49	6-factor	✓		X			
	5-factor	✓					
	4-factor	✓					
	3-factor	✓					
50	6-factor			✓			
	5-factor			✓X			
	4-factor			✓			
	3-factor			✓			

While neither of these two ways of constructing "factor" scales within this new data set resulted in factor loadings identical to those from which the treatments in this study were derived, there were some consistencies observed across these different data sets and different factoring methods. In each case, scales 2, 5, 6, 8, 22, 29, 30, 42, 43 and 45 – ten of the fifty scales – loaded on the first factor; scales 11, 12, 13, 23, 25, 34 (reversed), 36, 37 and 38 – nine of the fifty scales – loaded on the second factor; and scales 4, 14, 32, 40, and 50 – five of the fifty scales – loaded on the third factor. When there were four or more factors, scales 3, 18 and 19 loaded on the fourth factor; and when there were five factors, scales 1 (reversed), 10 and 46 loaded on the fifth factor.

Correlations between the three and four factors from the three- and four-factor solutions, respectively, and with the five equal-length "factors" and the original six STFB factors (those on which the treatments were based) in a sample of 695 inmates are shown in the following table. Correlations which approach identity are shown in bold.

Intercorrelations between the Various Factor Solution

		Three Factor Solution			Four Factor Solution			
		Factor 1	Factor 2	Factor 3	Factor 1	Factor 2	Factor 3	Factor 4
Three Factor Solution	F 1	1.00	0.54	0.53	**0.96**	0.55	0.52	0.48
	F 2	0.54	1.00	0.44	0.62	**0.97**	0.43	0.06
	F 3	0.53	0.44	1.00	0.53	0.47	**0.96**	0.40
Four Factor Solution	F 1	**0.96**	0.62	0.53	1.00	0.60	0.52	0.29
	F 2	0.55	**0.97**	0.47	0.60	1.00	0.43	0.10
	F 3	0.52	0.43	**0.96**	0.52	0.43	1.00	0.28
	F 4	0.48	0.06	0.40	0.29	0.10	0.28	1.00
Five Equal Factors	F 1	**0.95**	0.54	0.50	**0.96**	0.53	0.51	0.30
	F 2	0.54	**0.93**	0.45	0.60	**0.96**	0.41	0.11
	F 3	0.80	0.59	0.73	0.83	0.57	0.74	0.31
	F 4	0.67	0.46	0.72	0.59	0.45	0.71	0.65
	F 5	0.39	0.38	0.59	0.39	0.41	0.54	0.28
Original Six Factors	F 1	0.83	0.41	0.58	0.82	0.40	0.57	0.42
	F 2	0.73	0.68	0.63	0.67	0.70	0.62	0.51
	F 3	0.73	0.78	0.60	0.79	0.75	0.61	0.17
	F 4	0.21	- .01	0.50	0.20	0.01	0.52	0.13
	F 5	0.71	0.67	0.66	0.74	0.71	0.61	0.24
	F 6	0.77	0.60	0.55	0.79	0.60	0.50	0.36

As can be seen from this table, the first three factors from the three- and four-factor solutions are virtually identical; as are the first two factors from the three-, and four- and five-factors solutions.

The scales in each factor in the three- and four-factor solutions were then ordered by factor loadings (decimal points omitted), as follows:

Three Factor Solution

Factor 1			Factor 2			Factor 3		
A	B	C	D	E	F	G	H	I
5	Risk Taking	75	24	Zero State	70	50	Normalization of Criminality	55
42	Excitement of Breaking the Law	69	11	Hard Done By	54	32	Oblivious to Harm to Others	50
43	Extensiveness of Criminal Thinking	66	34r	Uniqueness	51	26	Denial/Hiding of Fear	48
29	Lack of Restraint	63	23	Lack of Trust	50	40	Failure to Consider Harm to others	47
8	Imperviousness to Punishment	62	25	Hiding of Thoughts and Feelings	50	15	Fear of Failure	40
30	Celebration After the Crime	57	13	Loner	48	31	Concrete Thinking	39
6	Excitement of Challenging Social Rules	53	47	Poor Decision Making for Responsible Living	44	14	Pigheadedness	36
48	Anger and Fighting	52	16	Lack of Interest in School Performance	41	4	Failure to Use Fear as a Deterrent	34
22	Lying	49	39	Ownership/ Entitlement	38	28	Focus on the Present	33
2	Suppression of Conscience	46	35	Fragmentation/ Splitting	37	44	Rejection of Fear (General)	33
21	Failure to Assume Obligation	46	12	Victim Stance	35	36	Refusal to be Dependent	32
7	Failure to Put Oneself in Another's position	40	27	Lack of Time Perspective	32	41	Building Up Opinion of Oneself as Good	32
19	Sexuality	39	37	Sentimentality	25	9	The Criminal Apprehended/ Fairness	26
3	Suppression of Fear (Specific)	38	1r	Voice of Conscience	21	10	Religion	24
20	Energy	35						
49	Ineffectiveness of Deterrents	33						

A	B	C						
46	Deferment	**32**						
33	The Psychology of Accountability	**25**						
18	Pretentiousness	**23**						
45	Suggestibility	**56**	38	Opacity/Transparency	**45**	17	Failure to Make an Effort or Endure Adversity	39

Column labels refer to: A = Scale; B = Description; C = Loading; D = Scale; E = Description; F = Loading; G = Scale; H = Description; I = Loading.

Four Factor Solution

Factor 1			Factor 2			Factor 3			Factor 4		
A	B	C	D	E	F	G	H	I	J	K	L
5	Risk Taking	**76**	24	Zero State	**61**	50	Normalization of Criminality	**56**	19	Sexuality	**52**
42	Excitement of Breaking the Law	**70**	11	Hard Done By	**60**	26	Denial/Hiding of Fear	**49**	18	Pretentious-ness	**52**
43	Extensive-ness of Criminal Thinking	**68**	23	Lack of Trust	**53**	32	Oblivious to Harm to Others	**49**	44	Rejection of Fear (General)	**46**
8	Impervious-ness to Punishment	**64**	34r	Uniqueness	**52**	40	Failure to Consider Harm to Others	**47**	3	Suppression of Fear (Specific)	**40**
29	Lack of Restraint	**62**	13	Loner	**50**	31	Concrete Thinking	**43**	20	Energy	**35**
30	Celebration After the Crime	**59**	38	Opacity/Transparency	**48**	17	Failure to Make an Effort or Endure Adversity	**37**	10	Religion	**28**
45	Suggest-ability	**55**	25	Hiding of Thoughts and Feelings	**46**	15	Fear of Failure	**35**			

A	B	C	D	E	F	G	H	I	J	K	L
6	Excitement of Challenging Social Rules	55	12	Victim Stance	41	14	Pigheaded-ness	33			
2	Suppression of Conscience	52	16	Lack of Interest in School Performance	36	28	Focus on the Present	33			
22	Lying	50	35	Fragmentation/Splitting	35	4	Failure to Use Fear as a Deterrent	32			
48	Anger and Fighting	45	36	Refusal to be Dependent	33	41	Building Up Opinion of Oneself as Good	29			
7	Failure to Put Oneself in Another's Position	44	39	Ownership/Entitlement	31	9	The Criminal Apprehended/Fairness	25			
21	Failure to Assume Obligation	43	37	Sentimentality	31						
47	Poor Decision Making for Responsible Living	41	46	Deferment	30						
49	Ineffective-ness of Deterrents	32	1r	Voice of Conscience	30						
27	Lack of Time Perspective	29									
33	The Psychology of Account-ability	26									

Column labels refer to: A = Scale; B = Description; C = Loading; D = Scale; E = Description; F = Loading; G = Scale; H = Description; I = Loading; J = Scale; K = Description; L = Loading.

Conceivably, meaning could be assigned to these various factors on the basis of the scales comprising them. However, we also happened to have available another data set containing not only the STFB but the Hare Psychopathy Checklist, the Sensation Seeking Scale, and the MMPI. Examination of the correlations between factors in the three- and four-factor solutions and a variety of other (possibly) criminality-related measures in this sample of 85 incarcerates again found the three factors in the three-factor solution and the first three factors in the four-factor solution to be essentially the same, while the fourth factor in the four-factor solution was highly correlated with the MMPI Spy (i.e., psychopathy) scale ($r = .95$) and Hypomania ($r = .92$) and, to a lesser degree, the MMPI Alcoholism scale ($r = .80$) and extroversion ($r = -.72$ with the Tryon, Stein and Chu Social Introversion scale), and with the DIS ($r = .74$) and ES ($r = .75$) scales of the Sensation Seeking Scale. Selected correlations for the three factors in the three-factor solution are shown in the following table.

Correlations Between Factors 1 to 3 and
Selected Criminality-Related Scales
(From the Four-Factor Solution) – 85 cases from Natpcl)

	Factor 1	Factor 2	Factor 3
Psychopathy Checklist - a	.05	− .54	.12
Psychopathy Checklist - b	.86	.30	.64
Sensation Seeking Scale: Boredom Susceptibility	.64	.19	.79
Sensation Seeking Scale: Disinhibition	.71	− .02	.72
Sensation Seeking Scale: Experience Seeking	.35	− .12	.35
Sensation Seeking Scale: Thrill & Adventure Seeking	− .19	− .54	.43
MMPI Anger (TSC V)	.52	.94	.07
MMPI Anhedonia	.19	.85	− .32
MMPI Anxiety (TSC VII)	.52	.84	.01
MMPI Authority Conflict	.41	− .09	.85
MMPI Depression (TSC IV)	.32	.94	− .14
MMPI Distrust (TSC III)	.67	.75	.55
MMPI Family Problems	.46	.56	.22
MMPI Habitual Criminality	.46	.70	.15
MMPI Manifest Hostility	.79	.69	.38
MMPI Overactive Thinking (TSC VI)	.63	.72	− .14
MMPI Paedophilia	.49	.90	− .13
MMPI Poor Morale	.45	.63	.25
MMPI Responsibility	− .88	− .35	− .56
MMPI Social Delinquency	.59	.93	− .01
MMPI Social Introversion (TSC I)	.16	.42	.05

MMPI Tolerance	− .76	− .83	− .36
MMPI Violence	.72	.70	.23

The following correlations are with scales from Quirk's Addicause questionnaire, in a sample of 82-89 inmates (S scales)

Need for Social Enjoyment	.12	.09	.16
Reactive Depression	.25	.36	.23
Stimulus Hunger	.60	.25	.50
Guilt Intolerance	.52	.50	.49
Social Contact	.14	.20	.18
Rebellion Against Authority	.63	.52	.46
Flat Depression	.44	.56	.42
Self Enhancement	.29	.11	.33
Hedonism	.22	− .8	.18
Subcultural Values	.49	.35	.53
Immediate Gratification	− .12	− .13	− .13
Affect Denial	.12	.11	.23
Need to be Different	.51	.39	.48
Rigid Morality	− .24	.06	.02
Paroxysmality	.37	.44	.50
Pep Up Need	.17	.07	. 21
Fast Lane Living	.64	.34	.45
Allergy Stress	.30	.41	.34
Physiological Anxiety	.34	.53	.36
Punitive Rewards	.54	.54	.56
Somatic Depression	.34	.49	.38
Substance Excitement	.50	.36	.40
Different Experience	.33	.36	.28

Examination of the scale contents of the three STFB factors and the relationships between these three STFB factors and the various other scales shown in the preceding table reveals the following notable components of the three factors:

Factor 1	Factor 2	Factor 3
Risk Taking (Loading .75)	Zero State (Loading .70)	Normalization of Criminality (Loading .55)

Excitement of Breaking the Law (Loading .69)	Anger (r = .94)	Oblivious to Harm to Others (Loading .50)
Extensiveness of Criminal Thinking (Loading .66)	Anhedonia (r = .85)	Sensation Seeking: Susceptibility to Boredom (r = .79)
Lack of Restraint (Loading .63)	Anxiety (r = .84)	Sensation Seeking: Disinhibition (r = .72)
Imperviousness to Punishment (Loading .62)	Depression (r = .94)	Authority Conflict (r = .85)
Psychopathy Checklist Factor 2 (b): A chronically unstable and antisocial lifestyle (r = .86)	Distrust (r = .75)	
Sensation Seeking: Disinhibition (r = .71)	Habitual Criminality (r = .70)	
Manifest Hostility (r = .79)	Overactive Thinking or "Autism" (r = .72)	
Irresponsibility (r = .88)	Social Delinquency (r = .93)	
Intolerance (r = .76)	Intolerance (r = .83)	
Violence (r = .72)	Violence (r = .70)	

On the basis of these results, it is suggested that Factor 1 be thought of as representing angry, excitement seeking, disinhibited, chronically antisocial irresponsibility. Factor 2 appears to identify an emotionally disturbed (depressed, angry and anxious), irritable, and distrustful habitual criminal; while Factor 3 seems to be measuring conflict resulting primarily from a combination of boredom and disinhibition.

Footnotes:

A search of the World Wide Web in June, 1996 produced only four references to "criminal personality," three of which referenced one (each) of Yochelson and Samenow's books while the other references all three together. It is hoped that these studies will make a significant contribution to the literature on criminal thinking and behavior.

REFERENCES

Akman, D.D., & Normandeau, A. (1968). Towards the measurement of criminality in Canada: A replication study. Acta Criminologica 1, 135-260.

Bhardwaj-Keats, A. (1986) Development of a test of criminal thinking based on Yochelson and Samenow's description of the forty-six thinking errors. Unpublished Doctoral Dissertation, University of Toronto.

Beck, A.T., Rush, A.J., Shaw, B.F. and Emory, G. (1979) Cognitive therapy of depression. New York: Guilford.

Blumstein, A. (1974). Seriousness weights in an index of crime. American Sociological Review, 39, (6), 854-864.

Bridges, G.S., & Lisagor, N.S. (1975). Scaling seriousness: An evaluation of magnitude and category scaling techniques. The Journal of Criminology, 66, (2), 215-221.

Ellis, A. (1962) Reason and emotion in psychotherapy. Secaucus, N.J.: Lyle Stuart and Citadel Books.

Figlio, R.M. (1975). The seriousness of offenses: An evaluation by offenders and nonoffenders. Journal of Criminal Law, Criminology, and Police Science, 66, 189-200.

Gottfredson, S., Young, K.L., & Laufer, W.S. (1980). Additivity and interactions in offence seriousness scales. Journal of Research in Crime and Delinquency, (Jan.), 26-41.

Hindelang, M.J. (1974). The Uniform Crime Reports revisited. Journal of Criminal Justice, 2, 1-7.

Hsu, M. (1973). Cultural and sexual differences in the judgement of criminal offenses. Journal of Criminal Law, Criminology, and Police Science, 64, 348-353.

Kelly, D.H., & Winslow, R.W. (1973). Seriousness of delinquent behaviour: An alternative perspective. Journal of Criminal Law and Criminology, 64, (3), 124-135.

Lesieur, H.R., & Lehman, P.M. (1975). Remeasuring delinquency: A replication and critique. British Journal of Criminology, 15, 69-80.

Maltz, M.D. (1984). Recidivism. New York, N.Y.: Academic Press.

Meichenbaum, D.H. (1977) Cognitive behaviour therapy. New York: Plenum.

Normandeau, A. (1966). The measurement of delinquency in Montreal. Journal of Criminal Law, Criminology, and Police Science, 57, 172-177.

Quirk, D.A., Nutbrown, V. and Reynolds, R.M. (1991) Sentence severity: A practical measure of offence seriousness. Brampton, Ontario: Ontario Correctional Institute Research Report (RR91-1).

Quirk, D.A. and Reynolds, R.M. (1991) Large-group treatment workshops. Brampton, Ontario: Ontario Correctional Institute Research Report (RR91-1)

Rose, G.N.G. (1966). Concerning the measurement of delinquency. British Journal of Criminology, 6, 414-421.

Rossi, P.N., Waite, C., Bose, C.E., & Berk, R.E. (1974) The seriousness of crimes: Normative structure and individual differences. American Sociological Review, 39, 224-237.

Sellin, T., & Wolfgang, M.F. (1964). The Measurement of Delinquency, New York, N.Y.: Wiley.

Velez-Diaz, A., & Megargee, E.I. (1971). An investigation of differences in value judgements between youthful offenders and nonoffenders in Puerto Rico. Journal of Criminal Law, Criminology, and Police Science, 61, 549-553.

Wagner, H., & Pease, K. (1978). On adding up scores of offence seriousness. British Journal of Criminology, 18, (1), 175-178.

Walker, M.A. (1978). Measuring the seriousness of crime, British Journal of Criminology, 18. (4), 348-364.

Wellford, C.F., & Wiatrowski, M. (1975). On the measurement of delinquency. The Journal of Criminal Law and Criminology, 66, (2), 175-188.

Wolfgang, M.F., Figlio, R.M., Tracy, P.E., & Singer, S.I. (1985). The National Survey of Crime Severity. U.S. Department of Justice.

Yochelson, S. and Samenow, S.E. (1976) The criminal personality, Volume I: A profile for change. New York: Jason Aronson.

Yochelson, S. and Samenow, S.E. (1977) The criminal personality, Volume II: The change process. New York: Jason Aronson.

ABOUT THE AUTHORS

Reg M. Reynolds, Ph.D., C. Psych. (Retired)

Reg Reynolds was born in Grande Prairie, Alberta. He attended London Normal School (for teacher training) before becoming interested in psychology and special education. He received his B.A. and M.A., from the University of Western Ontario, and his Ph.D. from the University of Waterloo.

He was a psychologist for almost sixty years. At various times during his career, he functioned as a counsellor and psychotherapist for individuals, couples, and groups; as Director of Vocational and Recreational Services at Lakeshore Psychiatric Hospital; as Chief Psychologist at the Vanier Centre for Women, the Oakville Reception and Assessment Centre (for juveniles admitted to training school), and the Ontario Correctional Institute; as a consultant regarding the assessment and treatment of sex offenders; as a consultant regarding ethical issues; as Coordinating Psychologist for the Central Region of the Ontario Ministry of the Solicitor General and Correctional Services; as a researcher; as a college lecturer; as an intern in, clinical member of, and board member of the Halton Centre for Childhood Sexual Abuse; as an intern, co-therapist and therapist in the treatment of spousal abuse; as a member of the Council of the College of Psychologists of Ontario; as a developer of biofeedback equipment and as a provider of biofeedback; as a student of education and special education; as a student of Applied Behavioural Analysis (ABA) and its application in the treatment of children with autism; as psychologist and Supervising Clinician in the Ontario Government's Intensive

Behavioural Intervention program for children with autism; as an educator of parents of children with autism; and, more recently, as clinical supervisor of ABA-based programs for children with autism.

He is the author of *An ABA Primer with Application to Teaching Children with Autism* and, with Stephen Bernstein and Alex Polgar, *Miscellaneous Musings*. He is co-author with Douglas Quirk of *Freedom from Addictions* and *Creating Peace* and editor of Douglas Quirk's *Adventures in Pragmatic Psychotherapy*.

Douglas Arthur Quirk (1931-1997)

Douglas A. Quirk was born in India, the son of missionary parents and, if I remember correctly, spent some time in boarding schools in England. He was educated in the classics, as well as in the classical English music hall ballads.

He received his B.A. and M.A. from the University of Toronto, and completed all of the requirements for his Ph.D. except for his dissertation – and he subsequently taught Psychology for Psychiatrists and Nurses in the U. of T. Department of Psychiatry for many years. He was a Clinical Fellow of the Ontario Society for Clinical Hypnosis, the Behavior Therapy and Research Society, and the American and Ontario Associations of Marriage and Family Counsellors, and he was a Fellow of the Royal Society of Health.

Doug was a prolific writer. His many publications included:

(1966) The Application of Learning Theories to Psychotherapy: Component Therapies and the Psychoses. Paper read at the Canadian Psychological Association Annual Convention

(1968) Former Alcoholics and Social Drinking: An Additional Observation. The Canadian Psychologist, 9, 498-499

(1976) O.P.A.'s Brief to the Royal Commission on Violence in the Communications Industry. The Ontario Psychologist, 8, Supplement

(1980) Nutrition and Crime: a review. Report
        Prepared for The Solicitor General of Canada
(1982) Biofeedback in Dangerous Offenders: Learning
        Normal Functioning of the Nervous System.
        Poster Session Paper, Ontario Psychological
        Association, Annual Convention
(1986) Nutrition and Violence. Invited Address, John
        Howard Society of Canada Conference
(1991) A Practical Measure of Offence Seriousness:
        Sentence Severity. Ontario Correctional Institute
        Research Report (RR91-1)
(1994) The nature and modification of criminality, Paper
        presented (with Reg Reynolds) at the Annual Convention of
        the Ontario Psychological Association.

At various times during his career, he served as consultant to the World Health Organization, (S.E. Asia Region), the Scarboro Foreign Missions Society (Toronto), the Canadian Institute of Stress (Toronto), Toronto Catholic Children's Aid Society, York-Lea Mental Health Project (Toronto), the American Society for Humanistic Education, the Institute for Applied Psychology, Humanitas Systems (New York), Biomedical Engineering Associates (Toronto), North York General Hospital (Toronto), and Green Valley School & Hospital (Florida).

From 1959 to 1967, he was Senior Psychologist at the Ontario Hospital, Toronto and, from 1961 to 1967, Director of the Behaviour Therapy Unit there. From 1967 to 1971, he was Director of Clinical and Research Labs at the Clarke Institute of Psychiatry. Briefly, he was in full-time private practice; and then from 1975 to 1995, he was Senior Psychologist at the Ontario Correctional Institute.

INDEX

CPSIA information can be obtained
at www.ICGtesting.com
Printed in the USA
LVHW041932260419
615749LV00001B/170